Advance Praise for
The Setback Cycle

"This book feels like sitting down with your friend who gives the best advice during your most trying moments. You'll finish it renewed, confident, and ready to take on any challenge life throws your way."

—**Jo Piazza**, international bestselling author of
We Are Not Like Them, Charlotte Walsh Likes to Win,
The Knockoff, and *How to Be Married*

"Through a combination of engaging storytelling and straightforward advice, Amy shows you how to work through your biggest setbacks and emerge with creativity, innovation, and a strong sense of self."

—**Eve Rodsky**, *New York Times* bestselling author of
Fair Play and *Unicorn Space*

"Every success story comes with setbacks. The key lies in learning the most you can when things don't go as planned. In *The Setback Cycle*, Amy Shoenthal offers a brilliantly thorough exploration into the fascinating science behind why setbacks happen, and offers an actionable plan that enables you to emerge gracefully from them. Just think how boring the movie of your success story would be without a few bumps in the road!"

—**Randi Zuckerberg**, entrepreneur, award-winning producer and
New York Times bestselling author of *Pick Three* and *Dot Complicated*

THE
SETBACK
CYCLE

HOW DEFINING
MOMENTS CAN MOVE
US FORWARD

AMY SHOENTHAL

A REGALO PRESS BOOK

The Setback Cycle:
How Defining Moments Can Move Us Forward
© 2024 by Visionaries Collective, LLC
All Rights Reserved

ISBN: 979-8-88845-168-7
ISBN (eBook): 979-8-88845-169-4

Cover design by Conroy Accord
Interior design and composition by Greg Johnson, Textbook Perfect

As part of the mission of Regalo Press, a donation is being made to She's the First, as chosen by the author. Find out more about this organization at https://shesthefirst.org/.

Regalo Press
New York • Nashville
regalopress.com

Published in the United States of America
1 2 3 4 5 6 7 8 9 10

*In honor of Alice and Ben Nash (Bubbe and Da),
who overcame countless setbacks as they worked
to create a better world for their children, grandchildren,
and great-grandchildren.*

Contents

PHASE 4: EMERGE

set·back
/ˈsetˌbak/
noun
a reversal or check in progress.[1]

---

1 Oxford Languages Dictionary

Introduction

"It was a spectacular loss."

Not many people would use such a word to describe their own widely publicized political defeat, but that's how Reshma Saujani saw it. She reflected on her congressional race against then incumbent Carolyn Maloney. The race had garnered national attention as young voters around the country rallied behind Saujani, hoping the newcomer would unseat the long time New York City congresswoman. To Saujani, her opponent represented the interests of only the wealthiest Manhattan dwellers, while the district they were battling to represent was far more diverse in terms of socioeconomic status, race, and even geography—it went beyond Manhattan's borders into Queens. To many constituents, Saujani was more in touch with a broader swath of the community than Maloney. And after gaining the support of many high-profile New Yorkers and a wildly successful fundraising campaign, many thought Saujani had a shot.

Saujani knew it was a reach. But she held out hope. She waited for the results to come in. And when they did, it was a gut punch. Her opponent won by a landslide, with 81 percent of the vote. Saujani was devastated.

"After the election, it seemed like everybody was talking about it—and not in a good way. It was a very public spectacle of failure," Saujani recalled.

She paused as she smiled at me over our Zoom chat over a decade later. "But that's why it was so powerful. It was life-changing for me."

I was fascinated. I knew that Saujani's experience of campaigning and visiting schools was exactly what showed her how drastic the gender disparity was in computing. She learned that in 1991, 36 percent of college graduates who earned bachelors degrees in computer science were women, a stat that dropped to 21 percent over the course of a generation.[1] And according to Saujani, the biggest drop off was happening with girls between the ages of thirteen and seventeen. Saujani was determined to find a way to reverse that trend.

That's what led her to create the nonprofit Girls Who Code, an organization dedicated to helping young girls everywhere learn how to code as a way of bridging the gender gap in STEM. As of 2022, the organization had worked to educate half a million girls.

As she shared more details about her journey with me, I couldn't get past that knowing smile. Was Saujani looking back on her "spectacular loss" fondly?

"If I didn't lose in that way, I don't think I ever would've started Girls Who Code," she said. "It made me realize that failure won't break you. You can try really hard things—things that you might not be an expert on."

Over the years, I have interviewed hundreds of founders and business leaders like Saujani. When their faces light up and they start talking excitedly, that's usually the moment they start sharing the transformational experience of what they did following a setback. This is so often the pinnacle moment of their journey. In almost every telling, what they learn during these dark moments is the thing that leads to their most brilliant ideas and often their most successful ventures. From Stacy London, who lost both her father and her career in the same year, to Amanda Goetz, who quit her full-time job to start a cannabis company while navigating a divorce and being the sole parent to three children during a pandemic—they all took an unthinkable low point and turned it into a massive upside.

In speaking with so many of these leaders, I noticed that there was a pattern, a cycle they had to go through to get to that golden nugget—from acceptance to growth, curiosity to creativity. They were taking their own setback experiences and using what they learned to benefit society in some way. I wondered if there was a way to package it into a framework so others could see what I was seeing, understand it, and learn from it.

Oxford Languages Dictionary defines a setback as "a reversal in progress." It's when something has thrown you off course or bumped you unexpectedly backward. It's returning to a starting line so the path ahead is less clear. It feels murkier. So why do leaders like Saujani see setbacks as so transformative?

The Neuroscience of Setbacks

Following a setback, our brains gain a new dataset that programs the basal ganglia, the part of our brains that draws from past experiences to dictate our future actions.[2] It helps with decision-making, learning, and forming new habits. The basal ganglia is our brain's command center, and it's always being reprogrammed based on new data. That data guides our neurons, which dictate how we choose to move forward, even after a reversal in progress has left us blindsided.

Neuroscientist Chantel Prat explained to me that when we experience setbacks, our brains undergo a dopamine dip. It is a moment when things don't go as expected. But dopamine is a plasticity inducer, meaning it contributes to the brain's flexibility. So it's actually setbacks that sharpen our brains' agility and strength. A slingshot must be pulled back before the ammunition can be propelled forward.

"Many brains are hardwired to learn more from setbacks than successes," Prat said. "But the willingness to do this depends on how much someone might be trying to avoid a setback. An individual's brain might be designed to seek rewards or avoid disappointments.

Some people spend energy avoiding the bad things while others move toward the good things."

Prat has demonstrated in her lab that people who have gone through more setbacks are better at problem-solving and reasoning. She explained that they're better at knowing when they are on the wrong track. They course correct more easily. That new path ahead seems a bit less murky when you've already worked through the experience of being bumped back to the start.

Shaping the Cycle

Reshma Saujani's story is messy. As with all the stories that you'll read in the following pages, there is no magic bullet to turn setbacks into successes as all journeys are nonlinear. The stories dipped and curved and swerved and swirled, and every time one of these leaders thought they reached cruising altitude, they encountered more turbulence. That's why *The Setback Cycle* is a cycle. It's not a clean U-shaped graph where you start out high, encounter a dip, course correct, and slope right back upward. And even on the rare occasions when that does happen, it's never the full story.

If you zoom out, that graph looks a lot more like a never-ending S. An S drawn by a preschooler who is first learning to write. The curves are uneven, sometimes they're drawn backwards, sometimes they look like a series of messy squiggles, sometimes they're disconnected. The small curves are important, though. The minor setbacks can be as transformative as the major ones. But when you're sitting on the floor among the scattered shambles of what could have been, you're actually in a chrysalis. Caterpillars rearrange their entire bodies in that chrysalis before they emerge as butterflies. They evolve into their new form. It is not too late. Your metamorphosis is underway.

Conversations with experts like Chantel Prat, several executive coaches and psychologists, and a deep dive into research around this phenomenon unlocked the reasons why the incredible people I interviewed persevered through unexpected obstacles and came out the other side. It's why I became so motivated to dive into the psychology behind setbacks, building a framework to gently guide you through your own. The Setback Cycle is the GPS that enables you to navigate these inevitable experiences.

Perhaps surprisingly, it all starts with admitting the obvious. Simply recognizing we're in a setback is the first step of a four-phase framework that this book explores:

Phase 1: ESTABLISH. How do you identify when you are in a setback? Some bonk you over the head while others are more subtle, building up over a period of weeks, months, or even years. Identifying what you are experiencing begins the process of gaining clarity so you can work your way through it.

Phase 2: EMBRACE. What do you do after you encounter that "Oh, fuck" moment of a new setback? It's important to give yourself grace and permit yourself to feel the uncomfortable feelings to fully process the experience before you can begin to grow from it—something that, again, is easier said than done.

Phase 3: EXPLORE. Once you've processed what happened, it's time to assess where you are, what you're capable of, and where you want to go. There are so many ways to climb out of a setback. This is where we start to explore our options so we can figure out where to go next.

Phase 4: EMERGE. This is where we move into action. It is by no means a finish line, since even the most successful people recognize that they are ever evolving because progress is nonlinear. Most people have multiple setbacks over the course of their lives—it is a cycle, after all. Emerge is that ultra important, coveted moment when you finally find yourself taking steps to move forward.

The Bullshit Filter

"This better not be some 'everything happens for a reason' bullshit," executive coach Shoshanna Hecht responded as I told her the hypothesis I wanted to explore. "Yes, success can come from setbacks. But you don't *need* a setback in order to find success," she said, emphasizing the word "need."

It's okay to acknowledge that some things are messed up and make no sense. Sometimes people experience personal traumas and tragedies that certainly should not be viewed as a "transformational moment."

Posttraumatic growth is the healing that happens after psychological, emotional, and physical trauma. While a trauma might be classified as a setback depending on the circumstances, a setback is not always a trauma. However, one may still find personal growth and evolution following a setback, even on the most subtle end of the spectrum.

A setback is also not merely an obstacle. A setback is what occurs when you've been working toward something, feeling like you're moving toward a larger goal, in a forward trajectory, and then something—a circumstance, a series of events, a societal shift, a relationship, a financial change, bumps you back to square one. Do not pass Go; do not collect $200.

"I don't think that people have to go through something terrible to be triumphant. But setbacks *can* be beneficial," Hecht continued. "It just depends on what the setback is and whether you can make a meal out of it. Do you have the tools, the fortitude, or the wherewithal?"

No, this is not a spiritual book about why everything happens for a reason. We are not here to glorify pain or romanticize suffering. It focuses mostly on business-related setbacks, although for some of these founders, it was a personal setback that led them to build brilliant, innovative businesses. I'm not going to, nor am I qualified to, go in depth about grief, loss, or trauma, which can be classified as but are not always necessarily setbacks. Mainly, the following pages will serve as a guide to help you if you feel like you have failed, are moving backward instead of forward, or are fixating on a mistake (your own or someone else's) and want to find a new path.

"I never considered certain experiences as setbacks," said executive coach Roshan Shah. "But now I find myself thinking about things my clients are telling me and experiences I've had in the past, and I can't help but see everything through this lens now. We can all come up with an example of a setback as it applies to the big things that happened to us. But it's interesting to think about the millions of smaller things that are happening all along the way."

Plus, in a moment where society seems to cycle through one setback after another, the following pages will offer a new perspective not only on your own life experiences, from the major setbacks to the smaller, everyday ones, but how they fit into bigger global issues and collective, universal experiences.

Societal Setbacks Can Fuel Progress

The pandemic was a societal-level setback for those of us over the age of four. After attempting to balance running a company with raising two young children, especially as both children were home doing remote learning, Reshma Saujani began to see how little society valued moms. She described the way the U.S. was essentially treating moms as, "the economy's social safety net." With millions of moms being forced out of workplaces, she kept waiting for action to be taken at the federal level to address the alarming situation that was dominating headlines.

She was in the midst of the Setback Cycle once again, along with every parent she knew. But because she had been there before, because she had cycled through a setback in such a dramatic fashion years earlier, this time she had all the confidence that she could certainly do it again.

Years after she founded Girls Who Code, Saujani ended up going back into politics. But this time she wasn't seeking office. Armed with the knowledge, experience, and determination gained from her prior setbacks—and successes—Saujani created a grassroots movement aimed at changing legislation. That's how the Marshall Plan for Moms was born. Named after President Truman's economic recovery plan that offered large scale aid to a devastated post–WWII Europe, Saujani laid out a framework that offered solutions for mothers who wanted to participate in the labor force, helped make childcare more affordable, and more controversially, offered compensation for the unpaid labor of being a full-time caregiver.

"It just became so clear to me that even though I'd been spending my whole life fighting for women's equality, I had been fighting to make the wrong types of change," she said. "Eighty-six percent of women in the workforce will be a mom at some point. That's how women's equality becomes at risk. This needs to be screamed about. It is worth fighting for and fixing and solving."

The Marshall Plan for Moms movement is ongoing and was renamed Moms First in January 2023. With her army of moms demanding change, Saujani continues to fight for paid leave, affordable childcare, and compensation for the previously undervalued and unpaid labor that powers the economy. In April 2023, those demands for change finally yielded results.[3] President Biden issued a series of executive actions that expanded access to care, providing more support to caregivers and domestic workers across the country. Saujani pointed out that this came at a critical time, with 40 percent of parents going into debt to simply pay for childcare. So many parents are paying more than they're taking home simply so they can work. That doesn't really add up.

She also noted that these executive actions would "directly improve thousands of lives among government employees and military families, while requiring federal grant applicants to expand access to care for their employees."

It really did seem like the lack of recognition and compensation for previously unpaid labor was finally coming to a head and being addressed at the highest level of government.

When I asked Saujani how she was able to power through setbacks so productively with such a clear vision of what had to be done, she didn't skip a beat.

Introduction

"I rise like a Phoenix from the ashes. I don't know any other way to be," she said. "My friends always say, 'Don't get in Reshma's way if she wants to get something done.' And they're right. We have to go from crisis to power, and we can."

You may be starting to wonder what the Setback Cycle could look like for you. Here's what it looked like for Saujani:

Reshma Saujani's Setback Cycle Snapshot

Phase 1: ESTABLISH	Over a decade following Saujani's public setback that led her to create Girls Who Code, she, along with every parent she knew, experienced firsthand the struggle of trying to balance her own job with remote school and a lack of childcare.
Phase 2: EMBRACE	Saujani waited for what she felt would be an inevitable plan someone must be working on to help struggling parents. After adequate reflection, she wondered why society seemed to be ignoring the struggles of parents, from those who worked outside the home to those who were sole caregivers, undervalued and undercompensated.
Phase 3: EXPLORE	Saujani realized no relief was coming. If someone was going to come up with a plan, she would have to do it herself. She researched previous economic relief plans and recovery packages. Eventually, Saujani decided to tap into her innate superpower of taking a situation by the reins and getting shit done, her efforts now aimed at solving this glaring societal issue.
Phase 4: EMERGE	Saujani drafted an outline for what would soon be known as the Marshall Plan for Moms, a postpandemic recovery framework that offered relief for working parents, and compensation to parents whose labor was previously unpaid. She started to see a snowball effect as she had conversations with local and state governments, even seeing some success at the federal level.

We are not all expected to be Saujani and come through the other side of our setbacks with such an extraordinary amount of success. Please don't think she coasted through phases one through four as easily as is outlined in this very brief snapshot. Plus, she was a savvy Setback Cycler by the time she embarked on the setback that led her to create the Marshall Plan for Moms/Moms First. But breaking setbacks down into these phases makes it more manageable—with practical, actionable tips on how to navigate whatever comes your way. While we work through that process, I'll take you through the stories of those who made lemons into lemonade. In fact, two bar owners did exactly that, opening an actual lemonade stand when their city of Louisville, Kentucky prohibited the sale of liquor at the onset of the pandemic.

The following stories show how leaders and founders emerged from their setbacks with innovative ideas, successful ventures, and creative solutions to some of society's biggest problems. Some are people you've heard of; others, you'll want to learn more about.

While these are the stories of a few individuals, their journeys reflect setbacks we've all experienced throughout our lives. Don't be surprised to see a bit of yourself on these pages. Perhaps they'll inspire you to realize that whatever you're working through, you have the tools you need to persevere and reach your own creative rebirth.

I am rebelliously optimistic in my hope that after reading this book, you'll see setbacks more clearly and emerge from them with a vision of all you can achieve. To go from wallowing to wondering. To ask yourself, *What more might be possible?*

PHASE 1
ESTABLISH

CHAPTER 1

How Did We Get Here?

When one hears the word "setback," their mind may wander toward seismic societal shifts. Emissions policies that undo decades of progress made around climate change. The rollback of LGBTQ+ rights in certain states. The June 2022 Supreme Court *Dobbs* decision that significantly rolled back women's reproductive freedom across the United States.

But a reversal in progress is not confined to behemoth social movements or Supreme Court rulings. It's fair to say that everyone will experience multiple setbacks during their lives. Some will be of a personal nature, such as divorce, illness, infertility, or loss. Others may be professional. Losing a job often feels like a major setback, as does losing investor funding or being forced to abandon a business someone spent years building.

Most people understand the concept of setbacks. But do we always recognize when we're sliding into one? While some defining moments hit you smack in the face, others are more subtle, like the stagnancy of staying somewhere too long. Sometimes it takes years for people to acknowledge they are in a bad relationship or a bad job. They find themselves floating along. They sleepwalk into a setback.

Defining a Setback

Setbacks exist on a broad spectrum. There are micro setbacks, which we experience daily, and life-defining ones. What one may consider a small hiccup may be a massive setback for someone else. The severity of it is unique to the person experiencing it.

Your surest sign that you are in a setback is stress. This often manifests as a physiological response. You can feel that primal stress move through your body as a tightening of fists, a clenching of the jaw, the tensing of your shoulders so they climb all the way up to your ears. Waking up in the middle of the night with a clenched jaw? You may be sensing a setback.

"When our senses pick up information," psychologist Susan David notes in her book *Emotional Agility*, "we physically adjust to these incoming messages. Our hearts beat faster or slower, our muscles tighten or relax, our mental focus locks onto the threat."[1]

So once we realize we're in one, what the heck are we supposed to do about it? First, there's the art of defining it. Naming it as you experience it makes it more manageable and begins the process of gaining clarity so you can work your way through it.

Shame researcher Brené Brown suggests we get through "first fucking times" (FFTs) by acknowledging that we are experiencing something we never have before. Organizational psychologist Adam Grant points out that once you recognize something as familiar, you can relate it to a prior experience and map out what to do accordingly. When he wrote a *New York Times* article about "languishing[2]" in year two of the pandemic, it went viral because so many people finally had a word they could use to describe their experience. Defined as the place between flourishing and burnout, the term seemed to give people a renewed sense of identity. We finally understood what this thing was that we were all feeling. It was so well received because the term and the explanation around it helped us identify our own patterns. It steadied us and equipped us with the information we needed to move forward.

Understanding when we are in a setback, as with an FFT, enables us to recognize it, create connections, and draw on what we learned to work through the current moment.

A Quick PSA: We Are Not Here to Glorify Failure

"The bigger the failure, the better your odds of a successful launch on your next attempt," Grant said, summarizing research on failed rocket launch attempts. "Organizations learn more from failures than they do from successes, because they scrutinize failures much more carefully, and they scrutinize big failures much more than they scrutinize small failures. When everybody is taking a close look at what went wrong and how to fix it, then you're much more likely to be vigilant."[3]

While it's great to acknowledge failures and learn from them, especially in high-stakes situations like rocket launches, we certainly don't want to go too far in the direction of glorifying failure.

It truly is wild to think that only a few years ago, Silicon Valley bros were being encouraged to fail big. Fail Big[4] is a concept reserved for those born with a certain level of privilege, who can afford a certain amount of risk. In the early 2010s, we were cheering on the "Fail Big" tech bros and the #girlbosses.

"We don't need to celebrate failure," Grant said. "We do need to make it safe to admit failure—that's how we learn from mistakes."[5]

The Setback Cycle does not glorify failure in any way, nor does it minimize pain, be it physical, mental, or emotional. It is a framework that simply acknowledges the fact that setbacks are inevitable and is here to guide us through them.

Grant's philosophy on getting comfortable with failure is based on the idea of learning from our mistakes. His book, *Think Again*, points out that there's power in being able to think and learn, and even more power in rethinking and relearning. That starts with acknowledging when we make mistakes, and having enough mental flexibility to course correct.

A setback is a moment where one is forced to rethink, and maybe that's the key to why it can lead to new, unexpected, even more creative and interesting places.

"Sure, our sense of strength often comes from success. But hardships can have that effect too," Grant said. "After big setbacks, people often come away with a greater sense of personal strength. They think, 'If I could get through that, I could get through almost anything.'"[6]

When things are going well, or according to plan, we are less likely to experiment or try new things. But as Chantel Prat noted, the more setbacks we have, the more rewiring and reprogramming happens in our brains. Acknowledging when we're wrong gets us on the path of figuring out something better. With that experience comes more adaptability and more of that much-needed mental flexibility.

This sounds hard. Where's the fun part?

...But Can We Really Derive Joy from Being Wrong?

Grant has spoken broadly about the joy of being wrong. What? Seriously. He claims that some of the world's most innovative thinkers, or the best leaders, just love being wrong. Supposedly, it rocks their intellectual worlds. This is something I really have trouble wrapping my head around.

You might be thinking (as I did when I first heard this), *No way in hell will I ever achieve this level of evolved humanity*, and maybe that's true! I'm also not convinced it's possible to feel joyful when we realize we've made a mistake, but sure, it is possible to understand the concept.

In *Think Again*, Grant encourages people to really try to embrace the joy of being wrong by reframing their mindset around it. "When you find out you've made a mistake, take it as a sign that you've just discovered something new," he says. "It helps you focus less on proving yourself—and more on improving yourself."[7]

It's not just about making mistakes. Of course we know we learn from our mistakes. We learn that at a young age. But a setback is usually not just the fault of one person. So if it's not me, it's you? What if someone else made a mistake that sent me into a major setback? It's their fault, so can I scream at them and tell them they are wrong and demand they find joy in this realization?

That's not exactly how this works.

Grant noted in a *How I Built This* interview that, "One of the most basic truths of entrepreneurship... is that the faster you are [able] to recognize when you're wrong, the faster you can move toward being right.... We should experience joy around being wrong."[8]

I have been wrong a lot. I have never enjoyed discovering I'm wrong the moment I'm made aware of my wrongness.

JOBW (the joy of being wrong) doesn't really have the same ring to it as FOMO (the fear of missing out) or JOMO (the joy of missing out) does it? Perhaps the acronyms are to blame for the lack of mass adoption around this movement.

If you want to practice being corrected all the time, A) marry a lawyer, and B) read a book or sing a song to a toddler who remembers absolutely *everything* including every song lyric and every word of a book she has ever heard. I have done both and this is why when the fact-checker for this book looks into my above statement "I have been wrong a lot," she won't need to go further than taking a seat at my family's dinner table.

I reached out to Grant to ask him about this understand-able-in-theory yet unattainable-in-reality state of human progress. I wanted him to elaborate for those of us struggling with this concept—how could we put it into action and practice it?

His response?

"Remember that the faster you are to recognize you're wrong, the faster you can move toward getting it right."

I was fucking wrong about the joy of being wrong.

I am often completely disarmed by logic. I will admit, I took a bit of pleasure in his response. I was the one who needed to do the work. I was looking past the obvious notion of the JOBW—that the joy does not arrive in instant gratification the moment the mistake is recognized, but in the understanding that you're on a journey to eventually arriving at something better. Patience is a requirement if we are to fully embrace this concept. Now that it makes sense, I just need to practice. To strengthen my mental flexibility. And I'm grateful not only to Grant, but to my husband and daughter who offer me ample opportunity to do exactly that.

My point is this: You likely won't enjoy being wrong at any given moment. Any joy that is derived from this experience will likely happen in hindsight and with the skills you developed from a prior negative experience. Negative experiences motivate us to rethink our actions, as our innate desire to avoid another negative experience can be powerful.

"People who are more accepting of their own failures may actually be more motivated to improve," psychologist Susan David points out. [9] Looking at things differently and acknowledging you may have been wrong, "doesn't mean wielding a wrecking ball," David says. "It means bringing history and context into the equation to find the full significance of what's there, and then putting that understanding to work to make things better."[10]

Grant adds, "Good teachers introduce new thoughts, but great teachers introduce new ways of thinking…. It's the habits we develop as we keep revising our drafts and the skills we build to keep learning."[11]

You can always find opportunities for learning, no matter who you are, how old you are, or what season of life you find yourself in.

The Setback Spectrum

Executive coach Roshan Shah points out that setbacks happen in two ways. "When we hear the word setback we think of these big, public events like Saujani's that lead to very big outcomes," she said. "But there's this whole other end of the spectrum in our microsetbacks— the ones that happen every day."

"We may not even realize these moments are setbacks until weeks, months or even years after the fact," she continued. "But every time we try something new, from that first presentation you ever gave to asking someone out on a date and hearing them saying no, these are also setbacks. We're constantly struggling through things and what we learn along the way is what collectively contributes to our success. We are applying these learnings to our lives as we move along, even if we don't realize it."

Shah, like me, began her career in marketing. Her words unlocked my own memory of what I now realize was a professional setback. It wasn't blatantly obvious at first, though things look much clearer with the advantage of hindsight.

The Motherhood Penalty

I remember looking in the mirror as I cradled my hands over my bulging midsection. At four months pregnant, I'd been poorly hiding my news from my boss and my coworkers. Until then I had enjoyed bonding with them over team happy hours and frequent boozy lunches (I'll never forget being served multiple tequila shots at noon on my first week on the job)—so many activities I'd no longer be able to participate in. I didn't want to admit that a personal milestone, something I was elated about, was likely to prevent me from thriving in this other highly valued aspect of my life.

I secretly, and perhaps naively, hoped my situation might be different, but I understood the realities of how a pregnant belly tended to send women's careers spiraling into downward trajectories. Ironically, I was in the process of being evaluated for a promotion when I saw those two pink lines pop up on the stick (okay, the three sticks) in the bathroom that January evening.

The motherhood penalty is a well-documented phenomenon referring to the loss of income related to becoming a mother. In one of her most widely shared stories, the *New York Times'* Claire Cain Miller bluntly points out that, "One of the worst career moves a woman can make is to have children. Mothers are less likely to be hired for jobs, to be perceived as competent at work or to be paid as much as their male colleagues with the same qualifications."[12]

She also noted how women's wages decrease further for each child they have. Different studies reveal different percentages for this: the National Bureau of Economic Research cited it at a 6 percent decrease in 2011,[13] while a 2018 study from the University of Pennsylvania reveals a 12 percent decrease.[14]

Regardless of the exact numbers, it's clear that mothers are penalized to some degree for daring to become mothers while working. And of course the decrease is even steeper for marginalized groups. There's much talk about the gender pay gap, but a 2019 study revealed that the gap is more of an ocean when it comes to mothers' wages versus workers who are not parents: sixty-nine cents for every dollar.[15]

In 1975, a manager told a Fortune 500 marketing systems executive he almost didn't hire her. He assumed she wouldn't stay very long because she would "probably have babies and want to stay home." But he saw her talent early on and ended up hiring her anyway. Sure enough, she had two children—and worked there for twelve years as one of their most valued employees. So valued, that in 1987 when she finally shared that she was planning to leave the organization after the birth of her second child, that same manager begged her to stay. They came to an agreement through which she would work part-time, three days a week (a structure unheard of in those days) while still collecting her full salary. On top of that, they offered her extra vacation days.

I thought of that woman, sitting in her corner office, how it must have felt to have the people who had originally cast doubt on her now offer her a part-time job for full-time pay and extra vacation days. Talk about a glorious victory overcoming not just a professional setback, but a societal one. She bucked the trend of working mothers and created a flexible work arrangement even before that term existed.

More than thirty years later, I kept a photo of her in her office on my desk in my office. In the photo you can see her sitting at a huge wooden desk behind a massive 1980s computer. Her striped button-down with cream-colored pants is an outfit so iconic that if someone wore it today they'd be seen as incredibly fashion forward. On the wall behind her is a photo of her baby girl—me.

I was hiding my pregnancy in 2018, not 1975. I wasn't alone. Many working parents still perceive caregiving as a liability in the workplace. In fact, a behavioral scientist at coaching platform BetterUp conducted a study in 2022 that revealed 32 percent of parents feel uncomfortable discussing their children at work. This makes sense. There's a palpable fear among parents that they'll be judged as unreliable, uncommitted, or unengaged by nonparent colleagues or managers.[16]

Staring at that photo of my mother, I was more determined than ever to work through this commonly experienced career setback. There was no way in hell I was letting my transition to working motherhood hold me back a generation later.

I got that promotion, beaming with pride as I stood in front of everyone with my enormous belly as it was announced. A display of career advancement while visibly pregnant meant I had emerged victorious over any potential bias or doubts around my continued commitment to my work. Surely this was the finish line and I had nothing further to worry about! I headed out on maternity leave feeling confident that I could overcome the societal barriers so many mothers before me had faced, just as my own mother had.

That victory was short-lived. When I returned from maternity leave, I was so excited to dive back in. I was ready to use the part of my brain I had to put on pause for the past three months and revisit who I had been for the decade prior. But things had changed in the twelve weeks I had been gone. As I was getting caught up on what had happened in my absence and attempting to reorient myself in the new balance of working motherhood, I naively expected everything to be exactly as I had left it and to return to my old role, working in the same way I always had before. I asked for updates on one of my accounts—the one I had brought in months before I went on leave and spent all my energy and far too many hours building so it would be a seamless transition as my replacements came in as I went on maternity leave. I had taken so much pride in what I built and how hard I'd worked to build it. And then came the update. I was told, in exact words, that I, "don't have to worry about that anymore."

I didn't realize it at the time, but the dismissiveness of that statement is what sent me into the Setback Cycle. I was excited to come back and "worry about those accounts again." Upon my return, I wanted to be challenged, to do something that motivated me, to prove to myself that I could still be the person I was before I went on leave. I had bottled up all my ambition and excitement and was ready to unleash it. I didn't want to be coddled. I wanted to move forward, not backward.

It's standard to shuffle the staffing on accounts at agencies every so often. And things change over the course of several months. Teams evolve. Plus, the people who had replaced me (yes I needed more than one replacement) while I was out wanted to keep doing the work they had been doing. Not wanting to deny them these opportunities or disrupt the flow, I was easily convinced that this was what made sense for them and for the business at the time. But where did that leave me?

It was hard to kick the feeling of being cast aside. Like so many working moms, decisions were being made without my input.

I told myself I should take the concept of "not having to worry about that anymore" as a gift. But in stepping aside to ensure growth opportunities for others, I had to tuck into a corner my own excitement to return to the work I previously took so much pride in.

I had spent so many years slowly climbing a mountain, and the second I looked away I was pushed back down. Why did I feel like I'd been kicked down that mountain while everyone else was partying at the top? Was this a caring team of colleagues trying to give me time to transition back? Or were they confirming my worst fears, assuming that as a new mom I was no longer as dedicated to my job? That my new baby was a distraction? Was it my own self-consciousness and desperation to show I was still valuable or were those fears valid? Did I really need to prove I was still willing to work hard? That I was still just as talented and just as hardworking as I was before I left?

Every time I dragged my huge pumping suitcase to the mothers' room, I worried it was a visible signal to my coworkers that I was distracted by my responsibilities at home, when in reality I was trying desperately to throw myself back into work. I got whiplash trying to figure it all out. Like many mothers navigating the transition, my return sent me spiraling into a complete identity crisis.

Mothers who return to work and want a lighter workload should absolutely be able to coordinate that type of situation with their managers. But on the opposite end of the spectrum, others who want to truly return shouldn't be penalized for that. My own ambition hadn't been removed from my body along with the baby in that maternity ward. When I confided my insecurities to a friend at the time, she told me this experience wasn't limited to moms. She, another senior level executive, had raised her hand to take on an exciting new project that perfectly matched her skill set only to be told that "her plate was too full" and she would need to stay in her lane, focusing on the work she was already doing. Those bigger, more exciting opportunities remained reserved for others who were perceived as more ambitious, less female.

I had set up full-time childcare, so in essence, it was almost like I wasn't needed at home during work hours, but I didn't feel nearly as needed at work. I sat in limbo, existing in the gray space as I tried to find balance. Despite knowing others who had done this, despite the zillions of books and articles written about this transitional period called the "fifth trimester," despite my own colleagues just down the hall who had navigated this experience before me offering all the support they could, I was unable to escape the feeling of solitude on my own island. I found myself questioning my value as an employee—something I had never done before. Society had imprinted this message upon me so severely that I was absolutely convinced that everyone around me was writing me off as no longer valuable to the workforce, waiting for the day when I would inevitably shrink away.

My setback wasn't obvious at first. This experience was in no way rooted in the overt pregnancy discrimination that so many working mothers have to endure, like Allyson Felix when Nike wanted her to take a 70 percent pay cut, refusing to honor the maternity leave protections she was asking for when she found out she was expecting.[17] But the subtlety made it more confusing.

I felt absolutely chaotic and deeply insecure. Why had I worked so hard leading up to my leave, staying late every night to make sure things were in order? Were the stakes as high as I was making them out to be? What would've happened had I left on time every night or if I wasn't bending over backwards to do what I felt needed to be done? Everything changed while I was gone, so was all that effort even necessary? What was I trying to prove? And who was I trying to prove it to?

Now that I was back, was everyone ignoring me or were they politely giving me the space they thought I needed? I kept going back and forth, wondering, *Is it them? Is it me? Is it them? Is it all of us?*

I had absolutely no answers, so I stayed quiet. I found myself, as Shoshanna Hecht would say, "floating along." With a smile on my face and a mind swirling, I froze. I sleepwalked into my own setback. Was this more common than I realized?

Floating Along

"What's easy is to float along and get swept away," Hecht said. "To say, 'this is life.' To keep doing what we're doing. This is what was happening for you at work. What I heard from you a lot in those days was, 'It's fine, it's fine, it's fine.'"

The impact is so often felt in those subtle moments, even accidentally. It is so easy to sleepwalk into a setback. Or to create one born of your own fears, your own insecurities, not because you've made things up for no reason, but because society has told you things have to be a certain way. And in my case, my company reiterated that societal message loud and clear. It's so easy to convince yourself that everything is "fine." That others have it worse. To see the good at the risk of ignoring the bad.

Think of how many people you know who have been in jobs, careers, or even relationships because of inertia rather than consciously waking up every day and choosing to be there. Think of how much potential they might be missing by not working up the courage to leave their situation and starting to search for a better one, difficult as that process may be. It's incredibly tough to choose that path. On the other hand, that's exactly what gets people stuck in a setback without even realizing it.

It is easy to dismiss these seemingly small annoyances without ever acknowledging that they may be the gear slowly shifting into reverse. When we are not dramatically flung into an overt setback, we can fall into these smaller ones. We either don't notice it, or we fight through it because we convince ourselves that things are not so bad, and others have it so much worse. It's … fine.

Turns out, one of the worst things we can do is fight through the Establish phase. It's counterintuitive to try to convince ourselves that it's not so bad, that we can keep going in the same direction, instead of pausing to acknowledge what might be glaring to those around us.

Psychiatrists refer to small transgressions, often occurring in the workplace, as "disenfranchised griefs."[18] They are defined as our small, everyday losses, the kind we as Americans have been trained to feel we have no permission to mourn. The field of positive psychology has created a societal urge to push away the negative rather than let it in. But if you let it in and acknowledge what is happening, you can face your setback head on. Mourn it. Work through it. Most importantly, you may find it sets you on a path that leads to something greater than you ever expected.

I had always taken so much pride in my work. I just had to find a new mountain to climb. I tried to figure out where else I could demonstrate my value. I felt, like so many do, that I had to prove once again that I was worthy of my role after what was perceived as a three-month casual sabbatical. I had to earn my place again. How come leaving to give birth, recovering from the physical intensity of it, and caring for a helpless new human seems to be perceived as more of a privilege than a fundamental human right?

Intuit's Angie Robert felt the same way upon her return from maternity leave.

"I was essentially starting from scratch," she said in an interview with Mother Honestly.[19] "You have to re-earn your stripes in addition to acclimating to going back to work, dealing with another child and navigating hormonal changes. It got me thinking: There's not a system in place for helping women deal *emotionally* with going out on leave, whether it's before, during, or after."

When one path becomes impassable, it's incredible what other opportunities can open up. The difficult part is being able to peer through the disappointment so you can decide where to go next. This will be a common theme as you read the stories of the founders and leaders who worked through the Setback Cycle.

I tried to figure out my own path as the number of opportunities once available to me at my firm shriveled away. I was no longer invited to boozy lunches. I struggled to join happy hours since I had to run home to my baby to nurse and relieve our nanny. Still, I wondered if I was imagining things. Maybe it was all in my head.

Years later, my experience was validated. Two different women from my department came to me independently, privately confiding to me on separate occasions that they, too, saw what had happened. They shared the same fears I had about becoming working mothers. Worst of all, their concerns had been exacerbated after seeing how I had been treated. One even told me it was a driving reason for her decision to accept a role elsewhere.

There was some relief in knowing I wasn't the only one who had noticed it. That it wasn't all in my head, or born of my own self-consciousness. I had confirmation that I had, in fact, been sidelined. What I went through was real. Others saw it too. Yet with that came the nagging feeling that perhaps if I had spoken up earlier, I would have been able to make things better for the women or mothers who might come after me. It was the opposite of the progress I so badly hoped to see.

I turned, as I always do during times of confusion, to writing. For me, the answers always reveal themselves on the page. Throughout my career, I had always maintained a little freelance writing hobby on the side. The month I returned to work, I had just published an article about fair trade that went viral, and has since been cited in research papers and articles around the world. With the increase in visibility came more opportunities. So I directed my energy toward my favorite hobby. It's not a coincidence that my freelance writing career took off the same year I had my daughter. When ambitious, energetic people are unchallenged, they direct their ambition elsewhere. The more I wrote, the more opportunities came my way. Soon I was interviewing senators, celebrities, brilliant entrepreneurs—trailblazers across industries. That little hobby that had always hummed along in the background took center stage.

All this time, I had been looking in the wrong place for validation. That writing hobby was the very thing that helped me work through my setback. It built up my confidence, reminded me that I was talented, worthy, and capable of striving for things that once seemed out of reach. And I was no longer suffering from what author Aliza Licht calls, "last name syndrome," the phenomenon when people start calling you by your first name and then your place of employment. It's what happens when your identity gets caught up in your full-time job, something so many of us, myself included, have fallen prey to. Writing led to speaking engagements, freelance consulting opportunities, an expansive community and more.

Once I finally named what was happening and acknowledged my experience for the defining moment it was, I built my confidence, and my career, back up, slowly finding balance as a working mom, toggling among marketing consulting, ghostwriting, freelance writing and, well, writing this book. This rapidly expanding "side hustle," as the kids call it, turned out to be a wonderful safety net, as I was, perhaps unsurprisingly, included in a round of layoffs only a few years later.

By the time I was informed of my employment status on that warm June morning, I had already built an entire career outside of my day job. My LLC had been formed, the website was live, and a handful of clients had already been secured. The folks in the meeting remarked how incredibly well I was taking the news.

As my work email was deactivated and the day's calendar suddenly cleared up, I shut my laptop and stood up from my dining room table. I paced back and forth, waiting for tears that never came. As I looked out the window, a smile spread across my face. Here I was, after years of researching setbacks, experiencing one of the most common career setbacks people endure. But this didn't feel like the *Establish* phase.

Getting laid off wasn't a setback—at least not for me, not at the time. Instead, it was a green light to move forward. I may not have realized it until that moment, but I had spent years preparing for this. I may have sleepwalked into my setback after maternity leave, but once I woke up, I was awake and alert. By the time that chapter was complete, I had already cycled my way into *Emerge*.

We often find success in the most surprising ways. And it usually happens after a setback. The founders I interview tell me this all the time, but it's different to understand a principle in theory when it happens to others and quite another to experience it yourself.

My hope is that by sharing this story of a very common Setback Cycle experience, one where it's easy to "it's fine, it's fine, it's fine" your way into ignoring it, I'll help others identify if they're in one.

My Setback Cycle Snapshot

Phase 1: ESTABLISH	I came back to work as a new mom, struggling to find balance and navigate a new identity. Confused about where to direct my energy, at home, at work, or some combination of both, I allowed myself to float along, convincing myself everything was fine and pretending I wasn't struggling to find my place.
Phase 2: EMBRACE	It eventually became clear that I needed to stop ignoring my discomfort. It didn't matter why, or how it was happening, I was stuck in a freeze and needed to find a way to thaw out.
Phase 3: EXPLORE	I looked around my workplace to find new opportunities and turned, as I always did, to writing. The answers, for me, often revealed themselves on the page.
Phase 4: EMERGE	In retrospect, I realized my internal alarm clock had been ringing for quite some time. It took years, but I found a way to feel valued again—this time, not so much from external validation but within myself. It came from exploring passions outside of the day job I had previously given everything to. I somehow found a healthy balance between motherhood, working, and writing on the side. I reflected on my setback journey. I started seeing the stories of setbacks in the journeys of all the founders and leaders I interviewed. I began talking to experts about this phenomenon. I wrote this book.

While some of us sleepwalk into a setback, or experience one so subtle we can deny its existence, on the other end of the spectrum, some of us are dramatically thrust into situations far beyond our control.

Rebuilding the Riveter

Amy Nelson created a network of women's workspaces, The Riveter, back in 2017. Nelson was in the middle of raising over $30 million in funding, had opened eleven spaces throughout the country, and was primed for explosive growth on the heels of a wildly successful Riveter Summit that brought together powerful leaders like political icon Stacey Abrams and soccer legend Abby Wambach in fall 2019.

At the onset of the pandemic, as coworking spaces took a major hit, Nelson had to break all those leases. She was forced to close every single location and completely rethink everything she had built. But closing The Riveter wasn't Amy's Nelson's life-altering setback. That happened a month later.

Early one morning in April 2020, there was a knock at her door. She opened it to find two armed FBI agents standing there. They entered her house and told her husband he was the target of a federal investigation.

"That moment changed my family's life," she said. "The government seized all our assets. We had to sell our house and move our four children multiple times through some of the scariest Covid waves."[20]

The crimes that Nelson's husband, Carl, was being accused of by his former employer, Amazon, included violating federal law, fraud, money laundering, a breach of contract, and more. He had been scouting land for the company to buy and build data centers on, which frequently required making deals with commercial real estate developers. Amazon claimed that Carl had inflated lease prices to gain profits that would then be distributed through a web of shell entities, including Carl's real estate startup. The company sought to recover tens of millions of dollars, an amount the Nelsons did not have.

I asked Nelson how she got through it. How could she possibly process what was happening, still pay attention to her business, and take care of her four little girls during this time?

"I barely remember that period," Nelson said to me. "The trauma that my husband was going through prevented me from accessing the creative and problem-solving part of my brain. It was hard for me to fight what was happening with The Riveter when I couldn't process what was happening with my family."

It's a well-known trauma response that our minds and bodies block certain experiences from our memories as a biological way to protect us. The physical reaction to emotional trauma can wreak havoc on one's body.

Nelson lost about twenty pounds in the two weeks following that FBI visit, and her hair started to fall out. "If you look at photos of me from that time, I look seriously ill," she said.

Nelson had a decision to make. She could surrender or try to fight. She could freeze or she could move forward. A phone call from her mother and the encouragement of a few friends helped her remember that she is, and has always been, a fighter. She mustered whatever strength she could and made the decision to fight.

Nelson told me she pushed herself to accomplish only a few small tasks every day. One foot in front of the other is what enabled her to slowly tiptoe out of her setback.

Because the government seized all their assets, bankrupting them, the Nelsons decided to sell their house and abandon the life they had so carefully created in Seattle. They temporarily moved in with family in Hawaii. Eventually, they relocated to Nelson's hometown of Columbus, Ohio. The North Star that guided all their decisions was simply the survival of their family.

The hits just kept coming, though. Two weeks after that first knock at the door from the FBI, Nelson was told her father would need a kidney transplant. This was during one of the scariest Covid waves, and she didn't want to risk getting her father sick. She made the heartbreaking decision not to see him as he was recovering from his surgery. Some time later, doctors found a tumor in Nelson's thyroid and she learned she would have to have a procedure done herself. Stress begets stress. Nelson's physical response was ongoing. Stuck in a spiderweb of setbacks, she was unsure if she, or her family, would ever find their way out.

If you've ever been in a legal battle, you've likely been given the advice to keep your story private. Nelson was so fed up with her situation, so tired of keeping things a secret from those around her, so ill, and so scared that she was about to explode. She spoke to Carl and told him it was time—at least for her—to go public. It was partly her way of processing what was happening.

Nelson started tweeting, TikTokking and furiously writing about what her family had been going through. She spoke candidly to the media. She shared details about the nuances of her case, using it as an opportunity to drive awareness to the overall issue of civil forfeiture. Turns out, her experience wasn't that unique. She started to shine a spotlight on cases around the country that had bankrupted families and torn them apart. For an issue that was otherwise given very little attention, people's lives were being completely destroyed by this system. Nelson was determined to speak out about it so that she might find a way to approach reform.

Meanwhile, she had her thyroid procedure and it went well. Nelson recovered at home. Her father's health began to improve. These small wins helped her regain her strength. She finally started to forge a path forward. I coincidentally spoke to Nelson over Zoom the same day she received word from the government that most of her family's assets would be returned. The reason was unclear, and she is still asking for answers, but signs were pointing toward her husband's innocence.

Nelson also began to revamp The Riveter. She leaned on her community, partnering with an old colleague and several old friends to expand the company in a way that addressed a newly evolved, post-pandemic workforce, with a jobs database, an education platform that offered courses and training from experts across industries, and Riveter Spaces, which enabled people to book coworking spaces in hotels around the country.

Nelson was certainly learning every day—about civil forfeiture, about the power big corporations hold on individual families, about how she might be able to rebuild her own organization, and what she as a human was capable of.

"Rock bottom taught me that I can survive almost anything, and that's given me power beyond anything I could have imagined," Nelson said. "Send your hits, disappointments, and bullets. I'll keep getting back up and fighting forward. You can't kill what won't give up."

Three years, almost to the day of that fateful FBI visit to her Seattle home, Nelson learned that the judge in her family's lawsuit ruled against Amazon, in favor of her husband, in almost every single claim they made. No criminal trial was needed.

Could it be?

"The judge tossed out the racketeering claims, fraud claims, breach of the Amazon employment contract, unjust enrichment, and more," she said. "Justice has been slow—and it cost us almost everything. No one should have to survive this. And I still have many unanswered questions."

Despite that extraordinary win, Nelson is still battling Amazon's deep bench of lawyers. Nelson continues to fight for her family's survival while working tirelessly to rebuild her business. As someone still knee-deep in the throes of her setback, her next steps aren't clear just yet. But it's slowly coming into focus as she works through the Setback Cycle, and Nelson is pretty sure it involves advocating for civil forfeiture reform.

"When you're stripped down to the studs, there's nowhere else to go," she said. "If you're going through hell, as long as you just keep going, you might get to the other side of it."

Amy Nelson Setback Cycle Snapshot

Phase 1: ESTABLISH	As Nelson tries to salvage her shattered company in the wake of the pandemic, armed FBI agents knock on her door, enter her home, accuse her husband of a crime, and seize all her family's assets. This defining moment signals a significant setback for Nelson and her family.
Phase 2: EMBRACE	Nelson falls into a deep depression. She goes into a long period of rumination. Her trauma impacts her physical health. Friends and family remind her to keep going and she begins to pick herself up and look forward. Nelson and her husband try to figure out what to do without access to the money the government seized.
Phase 3: EXPLORE	The Nelsons make the heartbreaking decision to move their family thousands of miles away to be near her in-laws. She starts to regain her strength and pushes herself to accomplish small tasks while managing to take care of her children. Despite being in primal survival mode, she remembers that she's a fighter and she's scrappy.
Phase 4: EMERGE	Nelson is still in this phase, but she's had a few wins that make her optimistic for her family's future. She's taken steps toward rebuilding her business. She isn't sure what happens next, but she knows it will involve advocating for civil forfeiture reform.

So, We Established We're in Setback. Now What?

So what do we do if we suddenly find ourselves in the throes of an obvious, life-altering setback like Amy Nelson's? On the other end of the spectrum, how do we wake ourselves up to make sure we're not sleepwalking into one?

In the *Establish* phase, you likely fall into one of these three categories:

1. You don't recognize that you're in a setback.
2. You deny that you're in one.
3. You are abruptly thrown into one that flips your world
   on its axis.

While Amy Nelson is a prime example of the third, my slow, subtle setback may toggle between the first two categories. The *Establish* phase can last for an extraordinarily long period if you never acknowledge that you're in it.

There are no universal criteria for setbacks. Despite the majority of Americans who saw the Supreme Court decision to remove the federally protected right to access reproductive care as a setback—a reversal in progress—there was still a statistically significant number of people who saw that decision as progress.[21] The same goes for personal setbacks—someone given less responsibility after maternity leave might see that as a gift, whereas I saw it as a setback. Most people see losing their job as a setback, but in my case, that moment felt like the pebble in the slingshot that had been pulling me back was finally released, propelling me forward. So what do we do with a lack of criteria around how to *Establish* your setback?

If you think you are embarking on one, consider why you feel that way. Are you curious about whether you should leave your current job? Some people take years to make this decision, only to look back and think, why didn't I leave earlier? You undoubtedly know someone who finally broke up with their partner, thinking you'd be shocked by the news, only to have your reaction be, "Glad you finally came to your senses." Maybe the one who finally came to their senses was you.

In the obvious versions of setbacks, we need to figure out how to put one foot in front of the other as we process what has happened. For the less obvious ones, it's time to get out of denial and stop pushing away our feelings to convince ourselves that everything is fine. How do we wake ourselves up earlier so we can get out of bad situations faster and start addressing whatever it is that needs changing?

Here's what I call the Alarm Clock Checklist, intended to wake up if you think you might be sleepwalking through a setback. It also allows you to take stock of your situation if you've just been bonked over the head by a big one.

Alarm Clock Checklist

- Every day (or a minimum of three days a week if every day is not possible), rate your motivation on a scale of one to ten.
- Now rate your mood (happy, sad, angry, burned out, languishing, bored, and so forth).
- List your activities for the day.
- Draw any obvious connections you see on one given day.

After a month, look back on your motivation scale and your mood ratings. Now see if you can draw patterns based on what activities surround any low scores. For your mood, see what words pop up most frequently.

Next, ask yourself the following questions:

- What are you most energized by?
- What are you disengaged with?
- Are you where you are because of a conscious decision to be there, or because of inertia?
- Are there any common themes that seem to be causing you undue stress?
- What can you acknowledge even if you can't act on it or solve it right now?

Remember that especially in the *Establish* phase, it's less about preventing setbacks (sometimes, they're unavoidable) and more about identifying them, even when they're hard to recognize.

If you have identified a common source of stress, a pattern or theme as you started reading, can you trace it back to some factor in your life that you'd like to change? Perhaps you've been hesitant to change because it's simply easier not to? Does something in your life feel like it's tugging at the literal definition of a setback?

If so, I hate to break it to you, but you, dear reader, have *established* that you are in a setback. You probably knew this on some level, which is why you picked up this book. That being said, I have some good news for you.

"All periods of intensity eventually end," Shoshanna Hecht told me during one of our interviews, as I scribbled her words onto a Post-it and taped it to my laptop. There's a way to navigate that period of intensity to get the clarity you need and the motivation to build from the ashes.

So now that we know we're here, can we fast-forward to that phoenix moment? Unfortunately there is no skipping ahead. Working through a setback requires patience. Next we have to *Embrace* what's happening so we can start to understand it. In Phase 2 of the Setback Cycle, we'll realize, as I did, that embracing our reality isn't as intuitive as one may think.

PHASE 2
EMBRACE

CHAPTER 2

Pause and Prepare

It might feel difficult, in the midst of receiving bad news, to consider that something better might be just around the corner. It can also be infuriating when others try to rush us through that process. Well-intentioned people may point out that, "Everything happens for a reason" or, "Perhaps this was meant to be," as you're dealing with a negative experience. Though meant to make us feel better, these statements can often disregard someone's experience. We all need time to process. It's tough to see the window that's creaking open just as the door is slamming shut.

Even though it's true that most of us can work through our setbacks and come back stronger than before, that is very different from forcing positive feelings on ourselves. Sometimes, things just need to suck for a little while before we can move on.

Our instinct to try to quickly find the silver lining and move on from our "Oh, fuck" moments can be blamed on positive psychology.

Defined as "a scientific approach to studying human thoughts, feelings, and behavior, with a focus on strengths instead of weaknesses,"[1] positive psychology is a concept initially coined by renowned psychologist Martin Seligman. He created it after growing frustrated with his field's research in the 1960s and '70s that, in his opinion, focused too much on the negative.

Unfortunately, over the past few decades, this movement has been twisted up into narratives that move away from Seligman's original intention, instead trying to motivate people through "manifestations," and tricking your brain into thinking only positive thoughts. It gave way to the now often used concept of toxic positivity. Bad news: you can't "affirmation" your way out of a setback. If it's helpful and feels good, by all means, you do you, but no one is getting through the muck without a shovel. You have to do the work.

From Avoidance to Acceptance

In my process of trying to understand how people work through setbacks, I turned where any self-indulgent writer/anxiety-riddled New York City woman would: seeking counsel from my own therapist.

Dr. Michelle Casarella isn't the type to sit stone-faced and ask you "how that made you feel." She gives concrete, actionable advice, is blunt when she needs to be, laughs with you, and offers straightforward answers to questions.

I scheduled time to talk to her outside of our regularly scheduled sessions to ask her about my theory. She agreed that slow, subtle setbacks are incredibly common, and that many people often try to "it's fine" their way through it as I had. In fact, many people don't immediately recognize that they are in a setback until they are well into the *Embrace* phase, where they begin to process the experience.

Dr. Casarella pointed out, "Our society tends to look at setbacks as failures—something to avoid at all costs. People also tend to look at 'negative' emotions as things to avoid at all costs."

And yet, there is a middle ground. It might feel uncomfortable at first, but we can simply acknowledge those negative feelings and peek into them to see what data we can find. Why did something make us feel a certain way? What can we learn from that information? As we begin to analyze and understand why our setbacks impact us so power-fully, we can use that data to program our decisions.

"Our raw feelings can be the messengers we need to teach us things about ourselves and can prompt insights into important life direc-tions," writes Susan David in *Emotional Agility*.

It makes sense. When we're going through something suboptimal, we're paying attention. We're listening to the clues we might not other-wise tune into.

Pain is a breadcrumb. When we excavate our feelings, we dig up those directions. Think of emotions as "a neurochemical system that evolved to help us navigate life's complex currents,"[2] which is how David describes them.

One of the most important things we can do is resist the urge to rationalize or "fix" your feelings. "Just feel what you feel," said Dr. Casa-rella. "If you are disappointed, let yourself be disappointed. You might notice how it feels physically in your body. This is called emotional acceptance, and it can take time to refine with practice."

Emotional acceptance is similar to mindfulness—allowing our thoughts and feelings to be what they are without judging them or trying to change them. It's the state we aim for during meditation. Or if you're like me, the state we very much struggle to achieve during meditation. Sitting still and attempting to calm my mind is a more daunting thought than running a marathon. My mind is loud and chatty. So chatty. Dr. Casarella suggested I take a "mindful shower" since I struggle so much to sit and catch my thoughts as they flow in and out of my brain. There's actually a science behind "the shower effect."[3] A study revealed that 30 percent of people have their best moments of creativity and glean their best insights while letting their minds wander in the shower.[4]

Hey, whatever works for you. We need that data, so lather up.

"As humans, we have an innate desire to not feel," Dr. Casarella continued. "To go straight to the rational part of things, to question if our feelings are legitimate. To ask, 'Am I being too much?'"

Wait, I wasn't the only one who did this?

"This is especially true of women," Dr. Casarella continued. Of course it is. Every woman at some point in her life has been told she's being too much. She's encouraged to "chill out." To be less emotional. To put on a happy face. Wouldn't we all look prettier if we just smiled more?

That's why mindfulness is so helpful, whether you find it in a ten-minute meditation or in the shower. Taking stock of your environment, your mind, your body, and yup, your goddamn emotions. That pause, whether intentional or forced, can be incredibly productive.

A Collective Pause

Erica Taylor Haskins remembers March 11, 2020, like a movie montage of the best day in New York City. The sky was blue, it was crisp outside but not freezing, and there were little blades of grass poking through a crack in the sidewalk, an early sign of spring.

She started her day in Brooklyn by getting a coffee at her local coffee shop—Ciao, Gloria—and heading over to a meeting at the iconic Intrepid Museum on New York City's West Side. The Intrepid is a massive ship that was decommissioned for the last time in 1974 and is now docked at Pier 86 on the Hudson River, now used as a museum and event space.[5] Taylor Haskins was there that morning to go over the details for one of the many events her team was planning over the next few months.

Tinsel Experiential Design was the company Taylor Haskins started with two of her close friends a decade earlier after leaving her job at an advertising agency. "Tinsel started a little bit as a hobby and creative outlet, something we could do so we didn't lose our minds," she reminisced.

Erica Taylor Haskins comes from a long line of entrepreneurs. Her great-grandparents, Sam and Molly, both owned businesses in Williamsburg, Virginia, in the early 20th century. Sam owned a barbershop and Molly owned a café. Despite the region's history of oppression and slavery having been abolished only two decades prior, Black-owned businesses had been leading the area's economic growth and were central to Virginia's business development at the turn of the century.[6] That didn't mean it was easy for Sam or Molly, but through the help of their community, they overcame significant obstacles and were able to keep their beloved neighborhood spots prosperous.[7]

I'd like to tell you that it has gotten easier for a Black woman to own and operate a business since the days of Sam's barbershop and Molly's café in Virginia. But, like her great-grandparents, Taylor Haskins had overcome significant barriers to get to this point. Despite the fact that Black women are more likely to start their own businesses than white men or women (according to a 2021 analysis by *Harvard Business Review*, 17 percent of Black women were in the process of starting or running new businesses, compared to 10 percent of white women and 15 percent of white men), only 3 percent of Black women-owned businesses succeed.[8]

There are several reasons for that, one of them being access to capital. And when you start to look at venture capital–funded businesses, the numbers are even bleaker. As of 2019, women-owned businesses still received less than 3 percent of venture capital funding,[9] a number that dropped to 2.3 percent the following year.[10] Unsurprisingly, that number declines even further for women of color. It's not that every single business seeks out or needs venture capital funding, but this stat is representative of the larger financial landscape and the tiny slice made accessible to women and people of color. Meanwhile, 20 percent of all small businesses fail after year one, and only half make it to year five.[11]

Despite the odds, by March 2020, Taylor Haskins and her company were seeing massive signs of growth, reaching a huge milestone—their ten-year anniversary. Tinsel had just celebrated by throwing a spectacular event at the New York Public Library. The event was called the Eleventh House as a tribute to the three founding partners' Aquarius birthdays, the eleventh astrological sign in the zodiac. As an added nod to their symmetry, they hosted the event on February 20, 2020. 2.20.2020.

As we all know, the arrival of Covid-19 in New York was about to change everything. Industries like hospitality, events, restaurants, and others that relied on in-person gatherings were forced to completely rethink their approaches to everything—funding, employment, revenue, and more.

With all the team's upcoming events canceled or postponed, Taylor Haskins had some unexpected (and unwelcome) time on her hands. She grieved for the events they had dreamed up that would never see the light of day. With the backdrop of anxiety, she found herself staring out the window, doom scrolling on Instagram, trying to distract herself while wondering about the future of her business, her industry, and the state of the world.

What she and others could never have predicted when they found themselves entering the Embrace phase was how much they were about to learn and grow from the experience. While her industry, like so many others, was devastated by the stay-at-home orders and suddenly quiet city streets, the forced pause had offered Taylor Haskins something she hadn't had since starting her company a decade prior—time. She wanted to use that time to learn some new skills and get curious about how she could potentially work to benefit her entrepreneur community, which, like everyone, was struggling.

She desperately needed to figure out what to do with all her nervous energy. How could she be helpful at a time like this? She had spent the past ten years creating in-person experiences. What was next? What could she focus on without her usual routine?

The Slippery Slope from Reflection to Rumination

Yes, it's important to reflect on your setback and sit with the uncomfortable feelings for a moment. Erica Taylor Haskins let herself do that. Perhaps she had no choice as she was sitting home with nothing to do. But she later learned, as many of us did, that a forced pause would enable her to focus on what mattered. So take the pause. See what you come up with.

But then, go do something else, preferably something more enjoyable. Obsessing isn't healthy, as we know. In their book *Burnout*, Emily and Amelia Nagoski warn against rumination, pointing out that it's not productive to continue "regurgitat[ing] our suffering over and over, gnawing on it to extract every last bit of pain. If you find your thoughts and feelings go back again and again to your suffering, ask for help."[12]

There is a delicate balance between reflection and rumination. Reviewing what happened and thinking through how you might approach things differently helps you learn from past mistakes. But ruminating over things you can't—or won't be able to—control, can be dangerous.

If you feel like your rumination may be turning into obsession, if you're experiencing low moods or nearing the point where you feel unable to cope, please seek professional help. There are wonderful therapists out there who are well equipped to guide you through whatever it is you're struggling with.

A pause can be productive. Just don't stay in it too long. But how do we work our way out?

There's integrity in walking away if something is no longer worth your time, energy, or resources. But we need something to walk toward.

"We thrive when we have a positive goal to move toward, not just a negative state we're trying to move away from," the Nagoski sisters continue. "If we hate where we are, our first instinct often is to run aimlessly away from our present circumstances, which may lead us somewhere not much better than where we started."[13]

> *As diamonds are formed by pressure and fire,*
> *from introspection comes growth.*

Shoshanna Hecht says the Embrace phase is what leads people to really pull back their lens on life and see the bigger picture, especially if you just went through something that threw you off course. "It's time for people to start having a completely different conversation with themselves on all fronts," she says. "That's how we start to play with what more is possible."

Pain is the absolute worst type of learning experience. But painful moments can offer a glimpse of what is truly meaningful. Don't ignore it. Fight against the urge to push it down. Thaw yourself out from the freeze.

Thaw Yourself Out

If you're still stuck in a freeze, focused on the pain or disappointment of what you're going through, consider the following questions:

- Did it teach you something about what you want and don't want in your life?
- Did it teach you some positive things that you might want to apply to future relationships?
- Are you blaming someone else for this? Can you forgive that person and wish them well?
- Are you blaming yourself? Can you give yourself a little more grace?
- What new information do you have?

Read that last one again. What can you learn?

"A lot of people get stuck because the next thing, the goal, feels too big. When that happens, we just become incapacitated and do nothing," Hecht says. "But if we can get people experimenting, little by little, then we're winning. If we can get people wondering, what more is possible for me at this moment, then that's progress."

Thawing from the Freeze

Regardless of the decision you make coming out of your freeze, it's likely that the road ahead may be uncomfortable. But that's how you get through to the next phase.

Taylor Haskins saw an opportunity to thaw her freeze when the Small Business Administration announced the Paycheck Protection Program. She dove right in, trying to figure out how to get the necessary funds to keep her own business afloat. Once she and her partners made their way through all kinds of paperwork and submitted the company's application, she decided to use what she learned to help her friends and other small business owners in her community navigate the complicated PPP dance.

"I like to say I got a PhD in PPP," she laughed.

Little by little, she was beginning to realize that one of her core values was to create things that were in service to others. Sure, she had built a career in event planning, but what she really had done was create ways for people to have joyful experiences. She lit up seeing the reactions people had to the experiences Team Tinsel had created. Now, as her focus was shifting, she saw a new opportunity to do what she loved, bringing people joy by helping them out.

Cycling Through One Societal Setback After Another

Her efforts to weave more activism and community-oriented efforts continued to seep into her work over the course of the following year. In June 2020, those efforts accelerated when a racial reckoning reverberated through society following the murders of Ahmaud Arbery and George Floyd.

The country was in mourning. Taylor Haskins remembered the day she heard about George Floyd. "It was such a tipping point for society," she said. "When it happened, we were still mourning Ahmaud Arbery."

Children in her neighborhood had made chalk art on the side of a building nearby that said, "Rest in peace Ahmaud." The morning she found out about George Floyd, she passed by it. "I was walking down the street feeling so heavy and heartbroken, and I looked up to see the chalk still there," she said. "It was such a sucker punch."

She remembers that moment as one where she just wanted to retreat. "I felt like I couldn't take any more," she said. "The layer cake that was that year just came to a head. I didn't want to talk to anyone."

Ironically, at that moment, all society wanted to do was talk to Black people. Taylor Haskins remembers how the cultural conversation and every post on social media seemed to be a panicked desire to "listen and learn" from their Black friends and colleagues. "It's this dichotomy of being like, yes, you need to listen to Black voices, but also," she paused. "Not now. We don't want to talk to you right now."

At the same time, the events industry was slowly picking up again after months of pause. "What we do is so celebratory and so fun," said Taylor Haskins. And this was the moment she had been waiting for. She was finally able to go back to doing what she loved, collaborating once again with her team to dream up beautiful experiences for people to enjoy. But that day, Taylor Haskins couldn't bring herself to have polite conversations with vendors and event production teams about lighting and decor.

Over the next few weeks, Taylor Haskins was invited to speak to numerous companies, sit on virtual panels, and host discussions and conversations at organizations she had never been able to get a call back from. "People I had been trying to get in touch with for three years or more came out of the woodwork, trying to check that box," she said. "So many brands came to us saying they really wanted to diversify their vendor list."

I could hear the eye roll in Taylor's voice as she told me this. When I asked if she was compensated for her time, she admitted that she was, but only sometimes. "I was happy to have conversations with people as long as it would manifest as a check!" she said. "But now, I'm kind of like, are they actually going to give me more business because I checked that diversity list? In June 2020, they claimed to want to diversify that list, but we're still here, we're still Black, and I'm not sure I'm seeing this pay off yet."

Despite her frustration and exhaustion, or maybe because of it, Taylor Haskins found herself at a pivotal moment, one that would empower her transition into an even more creative entrepreneur. Fueled by her frustration, the series of setbacks she encountered over that year, and a renewed desire to take on injustice and to hold others accountable, she started to seek out ways to bring this passion into her work.

*"At first it broke you and then it built you." —***Robin Arzón**

After spending the second half of 2020 having conversations about diversifying her industry, volunteering for causes she was passionate about, marching for social justice at peaceful protests, and helping her small business community navigate PPP loans, her efforts finally, finally, finally paid off. After a hard-fought pitch process, Tinsel won a contract to do an event that fueled Taylor Haskins' drive for social progress.

The upcoming presidential election was going to be a crucial one. Many, like Taylor Haskins, saw it as the potential turning point after what felt like an endless era of division and hate that was stemming from the Oval Office.

The contract was for a November campaign aptly titled "Pizza to the Polls." It was a multicity event that, as the name suggested, delivered pizza to people waiting in line at various polling sites. The idea was to turn an unpleasant experience (waiting in line to vote) into a celebration. And of course, to prevent people from giving up and getting out of line before casting their vote.

Taylor Haskins remembered how winning the contract felt like a pinnacle moment after a crushing year. "We never saw Tinsel as a vehicle of activism," she said. "Of course we all feel passionate about different topics, supporting women in business however we can. But this was the first time we used our event superpowers in a big social impact way. It wasn't like we came back and threw a great party, we came back and helped save democracy!"

THE SETBACK CYCLE

I could feel Taylor Haskins beaming with pride through the phone. She continued, "It's like all roads were leading here the whole time. We knew how to make it happen, but to touch so many people nationwide, in twenty-nine markets, the ripple effects that it had ..." Taylor Haskins cut herself off. "It was just such a great business comeback."

Erica Taylor Haskins Setback Cycle Snapshot

Phase 1: ESTABLISH	After celebrating ten years in business and defying the odds of being a woman, let alone a Black woman entrepreneur, event planner Erica Taylor Haskins was forced to put her business on pause due to the onset of the Covid-19 pandemic.
Phase 2: EMBRACE	With more free time on her hands, Taylor Haskins remembers staring out her window wondering what was going to happen next. She didn't have the answers, and she wasn't pretending to. She thawed herself out by reflecting on what had happened, what she had learned, and she started to wonder what more she could do. She used her pause to get clear on her values. She helped her peers navigate the PPP loan process so she and other small business owners could try to stay afloat, despite the closures.
Phase 3: EXPLORE	The country's racial reckoning fueled Taylor Haskins' passion even further. She started to explore how to build new experiences centered around activism.
Phase 4: EMERGE	Taylor Haskins found a way to combine her entrepreneurial spirit and event planning industry smarts with her newfound drive for social justice. She started with a new marquee event, "Pizza to the Polls," which encouraged people to vote by creating pop-up pizza parties around polling locations. She sought out other events with a mission-driven tie. If she was going to spend her energy going back to event planning now that the world had reopened, she was going to make a larger societal impact.

Erica Taylor Haskins could have easily continued to throw lavish events once the world reopened. But she harnessed her creativity and combined it with grit and perseverance, following in her great-grandparents' footsteps. And like them, she sought to benefit her broader community. She opened herself up to possibility and found new passions during her forced pause, all of which led her to her purpose: creating meaningful experiences for people and finding ways to benefit the community around her.

Tune In to Thaw Out

One of the ways we can do this whole business of processing our own emotions, specifically the unpleasant ones like sadness, anger, blame, shame, guilt, disappointment, and so on, is something as simple as sitting alone and listening to sad music. That very act can be transformative. Music is a connection point that opens you up to acknowledge your truest feelings, even the tough ones.

Erica Taylor Haskins remembers listening to a lot of music during her forced pause. Perhaps there was more to that than she realized.

In the book *Bittersweet*, Susan Cain dedicates an entire chapter to sorrow and longing, and in it, she explains the psychology behind why we love sad music. "Philosophers call this the 'paradox of tragedy' and they've puzzled over it for centuries," she writes. "Why do we sometimes welcome sorrow when the rest of the time we'll do anything to avoid it? A moonlight sonata can be therapeutic for people experiencing loss or depression. It can show us we're not alone in our sorrows."[14]

Cain talks about her love for Leonard Cohen's music and how his melodies and lyrics feel transformative whenever she listens. This spoke to me when I first read it. I have always loved sad music even though I am an incredibly (for the most part) upbeat person. I relish in melancholy melodies when I am sad, or even when I'm feeling super happy. I love Joni Mitchell and Sara Bareilles and I love their ballads more than any upbeat songs.

When I was twenty-five, my former roommate, one of my best friends from college, the person I lived with in my first apartment in New York City, passed away suddenly and unexpectedly. I had lost touch with her shortly after we parted ways, the guilt of which I still feel all these years later. If only I had stayed in her life, maybe there's something I could have prevented. One can never know. I fell into the rumination trap for way too long during that period.

One thing I vividly remember about that time was how I processed most of that pain by listening to sad songs with lyrics that would remind me of her. I would tell my other friends who were also grieving about the songs I was listening to on repeat, thinking it would be helpful. I shared lists of songs with them that I thought they would want to hear. I assumed, perhaps if it helped me, it would help them. And I remember the shock I felt when one friend said, "Amy, you just have to stop with the sad music. It's not healthy."

It felt healthy, though. I knew it was helping me, even though I didn't understand why. It was so new. At twenty-five, I had never experienced a loss like that. Especially the unexpected loss of someone who was also so young. The sad music is what allowed me to process my emotions after a situation that rocked my world—one that I was having difficulty comprehending for a very long time.

Cain also touched on the stereotype of the "tortured creative" and why that phenomenon exists. "Whatever pain you can't get rid of… make it your creative offering," she said.[15]

I asked Cain about how that could apply to the concept of setbacks when I interviewed her. "Maybe emotional setbacks instill an extra degree of grit and persistence, which some people apply to their creative efforts," she said. "Studies suggest that adversity causes a tendency to withdraw to an inner world of imagination."

Feel your damn feelings, people. Let sad music help you do it. In doing so, certain clues about yourself might be revealed.

The Embrace phase is a foundational moment in plotting your journey forward. Feeling your feelings leads you to finding stuff out. People need time to process a newfound reality and the burst of emotions that likely accompany a devastated dream—whether personal, professional, or societal.

Facing that stress, or that pain, head on is easier said than done, but a vital component of working through the cycle before deciding what action to take next.

What else prevents us from moving into action? That little voice in our heads that tells us we can't. That we're not good enough. That we're undeserving. Can you believe the shit this guy is saying?

CHAPTER 3

Name the Asshole in Your Head

A fun—or annoying, depending on what mood you're in—challenge you can pose during Embrace is to listen to that inner critic that sometimes gets in the way of moving forward. In fact, you can name it! Give it a goofy name and anytime you hear it, you can talk to it.

I'm not kidding. In fact, research backs this up. Using a third-person perspective can help you distance yourself from difficult emotions which often helps us deal with them.

"We default to certain ways of thinking," said Dr. Michelle Casarella. "We don't separate ourselves. Giving your inner critic a whole persona—a name, a voice, everything—helps you separate it. In the same way there's always one mom or one neighbor who you try to avoid because you don't want to hear them go on and on. Make the critic that person."

"We call it the gremlin in coaching," said Roshan Shah. "That voice in our head can be really harsh on us, and it connects back to all kinds of stuff from our childhood."

Remember, thoughts are not facts. They are only one piece of data but not the whole story.

"We need to remember that 'I am not every single thought that goes through my mind,'" said Shah. "Identifying and naming your inner critic and seeing it as a part of you, not the whole you, is extremely important."

The fun part? Get creative with the name while you defang that inner critic.

On an episode of *The Happiness Lab* podcast, Dr. Laurie Santos calls her inner critic "Linda Lamesauce," which is one of the best names I've ever heard. Emily and Amelia Nagoski, the authors of *Burnout*, call the inner critic, "the madwoman in the attic." Shoshanna Hecht's is "who d'ya," always whispering, "who d'ya think you are to do this thing?"

Mine is Mamarazzi. I call her Raz for short. She has a thick Long Island accent and talks in a low, raspy voice with a cigarette hanging out of her mouth. She's my childhood friend's unfiltered mom. She's always sitting on my shoulder, telling me I don't deserve things. She's frequently insulting my intelligence. Telling me that even if I was smart, or capable, that no one would ever see me that way. Also, she tells me I'm a terrible parent. That I'm not worthy of this job, this accolade, this title. This praise. Okay let's stop the onslaught, Raz. We don't yell at or tell our inner critic to stop talking. We simply find a way to live with them, listen closely enough to hear any helpful criticism, but shut out the unproductive parts that lead to self-doubt and fear. The goal is to get to a point where the inner critic does not dictate our decisions. They can no longer hold us hostage.

See your inner critic as a challenge. Acknowledge her and talk to her gently. Silencing her has the same effect as pushing down your feelings or trying to ignore them. It simply doesn't work. She will always be there, so learn to live with your girl Raz. No one will want to read this—*yet*. Maybe you're right. Perhaps I should edit it a few more times.

Erica Taylor Haskins was no stranger to that inner critic. When she left her advertising job to create her own company, that inner critic was loud. She knew she was capable of storytelling and creating meaningful experiences for people to enjoy. But her inner critic questioned her ability to run a business on her own at such a young age. I wonder how loud that critic was at Tinsel's ten-year anniversary party. Or if it enjoyed a slice at Pizza to the Polls.

Maybe, somewhere in there, we have another voice. Perhaps she's sitting quietly on your other shoulder, whispering, "But what if you tried? What if you actually succeeded? How good could it get?" Maybe we can ask her to speak a bit louder while Raz takes another puff of her Camel Light.

Hear her now? That's your inner hype woman. As you're in the process of working toward new goals and even new identities, your inner critic will really get loud. That's when you give your inner hype woman a goddamn megaphone. Tell me what I can't do again, Raz. I dare you. Today, I'm listening to Rhoda.

There was no truer hype woman than Mary Tyler Moore's fictional best friend Rhoda. Plus, her style was just impeccable. To me, Rhoda is the antithesis of Raz. Perhaps Erica Taylor Haskins' inner hype person—or outer hype people—were her business partners. Her husband. Her community. You know that old advice, "Talk to yourself like you would your best friend?" Surrounding yourself with real-life hype people is a great way to amplify your inner hype person.

"What is the positive self-talk that combats our negative self-talk?" asked Roshan Shah, "Recognizing that the negative self-talk is there for a reason. This is how our brains are wired."

Combatting your inner critic isn't going as far as to encourage toxic or false positivity. It's a way to name the thing that eats at you, that erodes your self-confidence. Use the criticism as motivation to help you improve. Let it fuel you as you strive to prove it wrong.

"I don't like the angel devil analogy," admitted Shah, "In coaching I like to simply ask my clients, 'What's another perspective on that?'"

She is quite literally coaching her clients to have conversations with themselves. I suppose that's the actual definition of self-talk, and it does seem like a great way to combat that pesky inner critic.

"Our inclination may be to go to the negative first, but we can quiet that inner critic voice over time," she said. "It's hard, yes. It takes practice. But it's not impossible."

Never Knocked Out

It's no coincidence that some of the world's most prominent fitness instructors happen to be people who turned to movement to manage stress after traumatic experiences. The world's most fascinating people? The fascination exists partially because they've been through some shit.

Peloton instructor Kendall Toole also used fitness to get through a setback, which led to a newfound mission of challenging societal norms and destigmatizing mental health struggles.

Content Warning: *Description of suicide and extreme depression. If you or someone you know are considering self harm in any way, please seek help from a mental health professional. The Suicide & Crisis Lifeline can be reached by dialing 988 from anywhere in the United States 24 hours a day, 7 days a week.*[1]

I spoke to Toole over Zoom one late spring afternoon. It was hard to believe this athletic, energetic, and bubbly person on the screen with her springy blonde curls and sunshiny disposition could have reached such a low point. She admitted to me that she kept some of her darkest days a secret for far too long.

Severe anxiety can often manifest as perfectionism. That's the trap Toole fell into throughout her teenage years and early twenties. Always pushing herself to levels of high performance in academia—getting top grades, excelling at sports, and filling her schedule with extracurriculars. She recalled how her positive attitude, strong work ethic, and cheerful persona did not match how she felt on the inside. "I graduated high school in three years," she said. "I was a cheerleader at USC, acing midterms and getting all A's. But behind the scenes I was really struggling with my mental health. I had two very different energies coexisting."

Toole, like so many of us, was trying to use positive psychology to get away from what she was experiencing. She was trying so hard to "it's fine" her way out of a depressive episode. She put on a happy face and overcompensated by overachieving instead of facing her demons head-on. And we know what happens when we fail to acknowledge our emotions. In the most extreme cases, this can get very, very heavy.

Just before Toole was about to graduate college, things took a turn. Her energy was waning. She was struggling to hide her true feelings. Overcompensating and overachieving had stopped working. She found herself at a new low.

"My senior year of college was when I went through a dark mental health period," Toole said. "I was at the point where I was contemplating suicide."

I had to ask how she came back from that.

"I saw how my decision would affect the people I loved the most, especially my parents and my brother," she said. "At that moment, I looked at my phone. My mom had just called me fifteen times. That motherly instinct? It is so real. Even that instinct with the people you love—if you feel like something's off, always reach out. Always trust your gut. We are far more connected than we realize."

Toole wanted to get better. But she needed help. She finally acknowledged how much pain she was in. She stopped chasing perfectionism as a way out. Toole's family cocooned her with support as she spent the following three months barely able to get out of bed while she battled crippling depression.

She was able to go through months of intense therapy multiple times a week to climb out of that dark place, slowly finding her way. Eventually, she returned to USC. She was able to graduate on time.

After graduation, Toole got a job at a hot new tech startup. Just as she was finally feeling better about her mental health, she found herself working in a place she described as having an extremely toxic culture. To release her anxious energy, she turned to movement, which led her to the boxing ring.

"One of my mentors was a film director who owned a boxing gym," she said. "He told me, 'You're intense,' and invited me to come learn how to box. That was a compliment, by the way."

"The boxing ring was one place where I didn't overthink," she said. "I felt strong and powerful there."

She finally left that tech startup and needed to figure out what her next career move was. Around the same time, her trainer told her he was starting a boxing fitness studio in West Hollywood and needed to find instructors. So she started teaching classes to try and lift her mental state, with the added bonus of paying her parents a little rent while she stayed with them.

That boxing gig eventually led her to audition for one of the biggest fitness stages in the world, a job as a Peloton instructor, where she now teaches boxing, strength and cycling classes. She speaks openly and vulnerably about her mental health struggles during her classes and encourages her students to seek help if they need it.

"I really connect with the imagery of lightning bolts," she said, her voice shaking a bit. I was tearing up too by this point in the conversation. "You have to have that storm, you have to have that darkness. You need that shadow part of yourself to be able to recognize the light."

The only way out is through.

Toole recalled a moment during that challenging time in college. Her father came into her room and said, "Listen, I know this is tough. I know this is knocking you down, but we will not be knocked out by this."

That saying became a family motto, and Toole famously ends all her classes with the words, "They can knock you down but they can never knock you out."

Kendall Toole Setback Cycle Snapshot

Phase 1: ESTABLISH	Despite being an overachiever and perfectionist throughout her academic career, Toole struggled with her mental health in private. She tried to "it's fine" her darkness away, using achievement as a cover for her struggles. After a significant mental health episode in college, she sought help from professionals and support from family and friends.
Phase 2: EMBRACE	Toole moved in with her parents and enrolled in intense therapy multiple times a week to process her feelings. Despite taking all the steps to protect herself, she couldn't escape her freeze and fell into rumination. She didn't leave her bed for months.
Phase 3: EXPLORE	She turned to boxing. She found that movement instilled a newfound confidence. Toole used it to work out her anxiety and maintain mental wellness. In fact, her love of boxing prompted her to pursue the sport as a potential career path.
Phase 4: EMERGE	That's what led her to audition at Peloton, where she now leads classes talking openly about her mental health struggles, inspiring and encouraging others to face their demons and work through them.

Identity versus Behavior

If you're like me and have a wildly impatient, very "what's next" attitude, and you hate pausing for even a moment, the Embrace phase might be the hardest. I get that it's important to be introspective as you reflect on a setback to glean what you can learn, but I'd love to fast forward to Explore when we actually start doing cool shit. To sit in Embrace requires moving slowly, exercising patience. I could say, "I'm not a patient person," but my drive to move quickly toward the next thing is a behavior, not my identity. I can untrain myself. I can sit still.

"It is hard to embrace that you've stumbled, or failed at something," Roshan Shah said. "This is where people can fall into shame, get really focused on what went wrong and tie the situation or the behavior to their identity."

Kendall Toole refused to let her difficult mental health moment become her entire identity. Of course, it will always be a defining part of her journey. But a defining moment does not need to completely alter one's sense of self. You are still you. Toole was able to acknowledge the difference, eventually becoming comfortable enough to talk openly about it as part of her story—just not her whole story.

Through coaching, Shah counsels clients on how to separate their behavior from their identity. "Not meeting a goal is so hard for people, especially ambitious people," she said. "They can get stuck in feelings of shame and connect one bad experience to their whole identity. I have so many clients who say things like, 'I am lazy,' because they didn't go to the yoga class or they didn't go out for a run."

"Embracing a setback means accepting that you're infallible," Shah said. "It's accepting that you will make mistakes, that you're not perfect. In that moment, we need to separate the behavior and give ourselves grace. A lot of people struggle with giving themselves grace."

We need to give ourselves grace as we work through Embrace. I love a good rhyme. Don't hate me.

Shah reminded me that while feelings are data, they are not directions. "Feedback is information, but it's not your identity," she said. "It's just a thought. It's not your whole you. While it's important to reflect on feedback, we need to ask, what is the story I'm telling myself?"

It's like in The Wizard of Oz when Glinda shows Dorothy that she doesn't need someone else to grant her wish of going home. Glinda just has the info. It's up to Dorothy to get herself home. But there's no way Dorothy could have realized that she possessed that level of power if she had been given the information upon landing in the colorful, terrifying, magnificent world of Oz. She had to go on her travels down the yellow brick road and experience all her adventures before she could truly understand the information Glinda bestowed on her. Only then could she realize she had the power all along, click her sparkly red heels and get herself home.

Kendall Toole turned to her family, and to intense therapy, to finally get herself home.

Our urge to ignore our feelings prevents us from gleaning the data our emotions hold. How many times have you looked back at a series of prior actions or reflected on a time when you were confused about where to turn and realized you had the power within yourself that whole time?

Movement Is Medicine

Humans don't like uncertainty and feel uncomfortable when starting something new. Even when that newness is exciting, it causes stress.

Let's talk about stress, baby.

"When someone confronts an oncoming car or other danger, the eyes or ears (or both) send the information to the amygdala, an area of the brain that contributes to emotional processing," according to Harvard Health Publishing's website.[2] "The amygdala interprets the images and sounds. When it perceives danger, it instantly sends a distress signal to the hypothalamus."

Then, the hypothalamus has to pass the warning along to the sympathetic nervous system, which functions like a gas pedal. This is where the primal fight-or-flight response comes from. The body gets a burst of energy to enable it to respond to the threat. Cortisol skyrockets. And when that happens, it messes with our entire system, including our hormones. It may also result in other physical manifestations like fatigue, rashes, and more.

Who can swoop in as the hero and stop this absolutely chaotic series of events from continuing inside our bodies? Luckily, our parasympathetic nervous system serves as the brake. That's the guy who finally waves the white flag, signaling the "'rest and digest' response that calms the body down after the danger has passed."[3]

It may sound counterintuitive in a moment where you feel like all you are capable of is crawling into bed or flipping on some mindless Netflix, but the best thing you can do to get that white flag waving is to move your body. Science has proven that movement and physical activity are the best things a person can do to break out of that rut. Common advice is to breathe, take a walk, or meditate. It's why Kendall Toole turned to boxing. When plans are foiled and the future feels uncertain, we need that rest and digest period before we can move into anything resembling productivity.

Movement can offer the clarity you're seeking as you try to pinpoint the primary cause of your stress or emotional discomfort.

What if the difficulty was reframed as an opportunity?

Or as Toole's colleague, Peloton instructor Robin Arzón often asks her millions of fans, "Are you willing to work on a weakness so it becomes a strength?"

She knows firsthand why that mentality can be so powerful. Two weeks before Arzón got her job at Peloton, she was diagnosed with type one diabetes—just as she was leaving her corporate law job to follow her dream of becoming a fitness instructor. But you'd be hardpressed (fitness pun intended) to find someone who talks more eloquently about turning pain into power.

Arzón is no stranger to pivots, firsts, and pushing through difficult moments. In fact, she began running shortly after a major traumatic event shifted her world. She was held at gunpoint during a night out with friends. She survived, but not without having to process the trauma of the experience, and a big part of that healing process was her ability to turn to movement.

As a kid who hated gym class and joked that she was "allergic to exercise," she found herself wanting to go on daily runs to "run away from my trauma," she said. "There's something *very* raw and empowering about just pushing your body to an uncomfortable place."

No wonder she often repeats the saying, "Movement is medicine." That's truly what it was for her—in its most literal sense. She needed to find that clarity that running would offer. She needed to complete the stress response.

Arzón's running journey started with a few runs in Central Park during blocked-out thirty-minute breaks in her work day, which set her on the path to becoming an ultramarathoner. The focus and determination she put into that hobby led her to where she is now, as Peloton's head instructor and vice president of fitness programming.

A vegan and ultramarathoner who was training for a fifty-mile race, Arzón was shocked by her type one diabetes diagnosis. She was in the process of shifting not only her career, but so many parts of her identity as she had transformed herself over the past decade. The diagnosis not only blindsided her, but challenged her emerging identity as a fitness devotee. Could an ultramarathoner and premier fitness instructor work through a diagnosis like diabetes, one that most people do not associate with good health?

She had to confront her new reality and the fact that she would now have to overcome some unexpected barriers. She considered society's visual of someone with diabetes. A moment like that could have easily sent her into defeat. She could have made her trauma, or her diagnosis, her whole identity. But after all she'd been through, after completing the Setback Cycle several times throughout her life, she knew what to do. She didn't ignore it. She worked through it and moved into action. By doing so, she was able to reframe her expectations not only for herself, but for millions of people.

She recalls how she simply didn't have time for self-pity. She had a race to train for. So she had to figure out how to merge this new diagnosis with her goals. "The first thing I asked my endocrinologist was, 'How the hell am I going to run this ultramarathon in three weeks?'" Arzón said.

She told me she stares setbacks squarely in the face and says, "Okay, this happened, now let's break out of the boxes society places us in and build new ones."

"Get me a hammer," she laughed.

Now Arzón proudly sports her insulin patch on every single workout she leads for the millions of people who tune in from all over the world. From thirty minutes a day to thirty million fans, Arzón now points out, "I had a choice. I could crumble, or pivot. I will always pivot."

Arzón ran that fifty-mile race and finished it. Then she ran three more, and another one hundred–mile race. No wonder she hypes up her riders in each of her classes by talking about turning pain into power.

Her advice resonates with founders and leaders worldwide—myself included, especially as I was diagnosed by my doctor with prediabetes as I was writing this book. Hopping on my bike and seeing Arzón sport her insulin patch helped me reframe my own perception of what that could mean. If you find yourself in a space you didn't expect, don't get discouraged—get creative, get curious, connect with others, and learn from it. After a setback, it's not really about bouncing back, but rather, moving forward.

Speaking of the antiquated concept of "bouncing back," I spoke to Arzón a few weeks after she returned from another scenario that blew her—and society's expectations—out of the water. Arzón was the first Peloton instructor to share how she worked out during her pregnancy so publicly, to go on maternity leave and show the world what that journey could look like. Reminding us she is human, she described her return to fitness postpartum as humbling. Since then, multiple instructors have followed her lead.

"I think we're moving away from 'stay in your lane,'" she said.[4] "We are creating a multi hyphenate existence, where we can be all the things. I'm a mom, I'm an ultramarathoner, I'm an executive, and I choose which of those are my primary identity at any given moment."

Arzón continues to set new expectations for herself, often exceeding them, and in doing so she's challenging deep-rooted societal norms. What does a pregnant woman working out look like? Can a diabetic also be an athlete? Can a lawyer be an ultramarathoner? Can a mom wear crop tops and spandex in front of millions of people daily? To Arzón, the answer is an obvious and resounding yes. She's shifting all our assumptions—and our expectations.

Robin Arzón Setback Cycle Snapshot

Phase 1: ESTABLISH	Arzón was diagnosed with diabetes just weeks before switching careers from lawyer to fitness instructor. She was also training to run an ultramarathon.
Phase 2: EMBRACE	She faced her situation head on. Yes, she was disappointed, but she acknowledged her disappointment. She didn't ignore it. She embraced movement, as always, to process what she was going through. And she also didn't let it define her identity. Even with her new diagnosis, Arzón was determined to reach that goal of becoming a fitness instructor and ultramarathoner.
Phase 3: EXPLORE	Arzón and other diabetics need to make what she says are "one hundred little decisions every day" to maintain good health. Tapping into her determination and perseverance, she put her insulin patch on while diving into research. She didn't want to simply function; she wanted to thrive. She figured out what she now needed to do every day to live the full life she wanted, even with her condition.
Phase 4: EMERGE	Arzón defied societal expectations of what a fitness instructor or athlete can be. She decided to talk openly during classes about how she worked through her diagnosis in the hopes of inspiring others. She now encourages those in her wellness community to consider how they might be able to apply this to their own lives and "break the boxes they put you in."

The Great Expectations Gap

As Arzón learned throughout her journey, managing one's expectations—and separating our own from society's—can be a delicate balance. Set them too high, and we risk disappointment. But aiming too low makes us feel like we're not doing enough.

What most of us don't realize is how much pressure we put on ourselves based on the expectations of others.

"As humans, it's natural for us to go into things with extraordinarily high expectations we can never possibly meet," Dr. Casarella said. "It's a vicious cycle because then of course we feel bad about ourselves when we don't meet those expectations."

So how do we close that expectations gap so we can still aim high while avoiding constant disappointment?

Morra Aarons-Mele is a bestselling author and the host of *The Anxious Achiever* podcast, where she has candid conversations with leaders about all the things that make them anxious. Aarons-Mele, who lives with anxiety and struggles with managing expectations for herself, pointed out in one of her newsletters that, "Sometimes, expectations that feel like your own are not; you might have internalized them as your own from a formative experience in your life." To figure out where your expectations are stemming from, Aarons-Mele suggests a straightforward activity to help close the expectations gap: an Expectations Audit.

Expectations Audit (by Morra Aarons-Mele)[5]

Start this exercise by asking:

- What drives you? Is it your own expectations, or the expectations of others?
- Are those expectations crushing you, making every day harder?

If your expectations feel overwhelming, consider setting aside five minutes to write down the following:

- A big milestone you've reached, or one you're currently working toward. It could be a specific job title, a completed project, a business goal, a salary figure, a fitness goal, or any marker of progress and accomplishment.
- If it's your own expectation, look at it again. What might you change?
- Ask: Is this an expectation I want to keep? Or can I let this one go?

Wow. How many expectations have I set for myself based on how I think something might align with society's expectation of me? My parents' expectation of me? Or alternatively, how have I defied or rebelled against those expectations? Rebelling against them is still responding to someone else's expectations, not setting your own.

Aarons-Mele says she uses this approach for managing her own expectations around her body and her relationship with fitness. "I struggle with my body image and compulsions around dieting and exercise," she said. "I grew up in a culture and in a household that rewarded thinness and excellent physical fitness. I realized several years ago that my high expectations around what my body should look like are actually learned behaviors, and that they'd become my own through a long process of internalization."[6]

My formative teenage years were spent in the era of low-cut jeans, Britney Spears, and glossy fashion magazines celebrating thinness above all else. Like Aarons-Mele, I have also internalized the idea of what an ideal female body should look like. And like many women, I have spent more mental energy than I care to admit, especially during my postpregnancy, metabolism-slowing entry into midlife attempting to unravel those expectations.

What Aarons-Mele eventually realized after going through her expectations audit was that her true motivation around physical fitness really aligned with her love of playing sports. "My own expectation is to have fun playing games like tennis," she said. "I'm working to remind myself that I love playing sports, because otherwise the other (physical appearance-based) expectation is so strong and ingrained it can dominate and suck the joy out of my life."[7]

Like Kendall Toole, Aarons-Mele considers herself a perfectionist. It's a core part of her identity, one that she has held tight to for most of her life. But she's actively working to let go of that. When she notices herself in a swirl of perfectionism, she steps back, and says out loud, "Hi, Mom."

"Striving for happiness establishes an expectation, which confirms the saying that expectations are resentments waiting to happen," says Susan David in *Emotional Agility*, "That's why holidays and family events are often disappointing, if not downright depressing. Our expectations are so high that it's almost inevitable we'll be let down." [8]

Chantel Prat uses the same logic around New Year's Eve. "Everyone has one great New Year's Eve party and then subsequent New Year's Eves are never quite as good, because they can never quite measure up," she said.

Anyone who has ever waited in a freezing line to get into a too-hyped, too-expensive ticketed New Year's Eve party unfortunately knows this phenomenon all too well. That's why so many of us tend to enjoy smaller gatherings in the comfort of our own homes. That, and who wants to wait in line in the cold when we can champagne toast from our cozy couches?

The hardest part of this expectations audit is acknowledging if and when you might be ready to step away from these expectations that feel like they're yours, but you now realize were set by someone else. That's when you have to figure out if you want to hold onto them or decide if it's time to say goodbye. This is really hard to do! Aarons-Mele grapples with this herself.

"My own expectations, no matter their origin, are always going to be ridiculously high," Aarons-Mele said. "It's just how I roll."

Aarons-Mele believes once we understand what drives us to achieve, we can change our life for the better. She suggests that the next time we jump to reach an expectation that's too high, we give ourselves a moment to say, "Is this something that I really want? Is it an expectation that is reasonable for me to take on?"[9]

And I would add, where did that expectation come from—your parents, grandparents, your community, society—or yourself? What if we went back in time a bit and reset those expectations with a clean slate? Like... all the way back?

CHAPTER 4

What Babies Can Teach Us

Have you ever been a baby? Me too. Do you remember feeling self-conscious or afraid to try something new when you were a baby?

No, because one—we don't start forming long term memories until after age one, and two—because babies are fucking fearless.

Oddly, as we get older, we are discouraged from learning new things. "I'm too far gone and there's no hope of me changing things now." Or, "Don't fix what ain't broke." You've heard people say these things. Perhaps you've said them yourself.

Adults have been trained to avoid opportunities for continued learning, mostly for fear of failure, or simply shrugging off the desire to try. We graduate from whatever level of schooling we achieve, find an occupation, and spend the first few years of our career learning that occupation. We achieve some modicum of success and start training others to do what we do, just as we've done it. Maybe we develop a hobby at some point, but honestly most of us don't even do that. We sit on our couch, tired at the end of the day, scrolling our phones or watching some streaming service. At some point, we train ourselves to stop seeking opportunities for learning. We start coasting. We spend too many years doing the same thing and think *I can't start over now.*

We propel ourselves forward by inertia. We just keep going even if we're losing our enthusiasm by the minute.

We sleepwalk into a setback.

Luckily, there are ways to avoid this trap. You just need to adopt the right mindset.

The Growth Mindset

Psychologist Carol Dweck literally wrote the book on mindsets. According to her, a growth mindset is based on "the belief that your basic qualities are things you can cultivate through your efforts, your strategies and help from others."[1] The growth mindset encourages you to improve at learning and stumbling, even as an adult.

In the fixed mindset, things are unchangeable; in the growth mindset, there is room to, well, grow. The fixed mindset offers outcome as the standard of measurement. The growth mindset offers the path of learning and the satisfaction of practicing until you improve as the holy grail.

A growth mindset doesn't happen naturally for many of us. In fact, many people get stuck believing our qualities are carved in stone. To people with a fixed mindset, your identity is what it is—you are either smart or not, athletic or not, artistic or not. There is no in-between. There is no space to explore, learn and improve.

Can you guess which mindset you'll need as you work through the Setback Cycle?

Why Babies DGAF [2]

One of the reasons FFTs are so scary is because as adults, we may be frightened of trying new things for fear of embarrassment. Making mistakes, looking incompetent, and feeling shame are incredibly strong deterrents from our attempts to learn. Getting over a fear of uncertainty can be debilitating.

Every time I board a plane to travel to a new country, I'm filled with excitement and a little fear. Even if I have my trip planned down to the minute (ask my friends about our trip to Italy where I had bathroom breaks on the schedule), it has always been scary to fly somewhere new where I didn't speak the language and could never fully know what to expect.

But some of the most incredible and transformative experiences of my life have been made on those trips. I remember conquering my fear of heights and overcoming what I saw as a lack of athletic ability when I climbed Huayna Picchu in Peru.

No one else seemed to have any trouble or fear racing up to the top. And then there was me.

How I struggled and huffed and puffed up the mountain. But I never considered going back. I paused to take breaks, letting the distance between myself and the rest of my party widen further. When I finally reached the top and looked around at the magnificent view, I remember the distinct realization of how nothing this rewarding ever comes without a little fear and a lot of effort.

It goes back to how we look at our identity versus behavior. "I am not athletic and I am afraid of heights." If I let that identity define me, I never would have climbed that mountain. Instead, I acknowledged this would be hard, but that I was fully capable of getting to the top. I may have been the last one to arrive there, but I made it.

In the growth mindset, failure is defined as a lack of attempt. Failure is pushing down your wonder of "What if I tried?"

You know who moves forward without any concern of failure or embarrassment? Babies.

"Babies don't worry about making mistakes or humiliating them-selves," Dweck points out, citing an often used but perfect example of the growth mindset. "They walk, they fall, they get up. They just barge forward."[3]

"Think about someone you know who is steeped in the fixed mindset. Think about how they're always trying to prove themselves and how they're supersensitive about being wrong or making mistakes. Did you ever wonder why they were this way?" Dweck says, before she bluntly asks, "Are you this way?"

Retrain Your Brain

Those in a fixed mindset allow their setbacks to define them and they give up easily. "I'm not qualified to run a business." "My body is not strong." Those who adopt a growth mindset are motivated to try again, pivot, and be fearless in their pursuit of exploration and learning. The good news is, a mindset is something that can be changed through practice, and it can help us evaluate decisions as we carve a new path forward.

You can also name your fixed mindset in the same way we named our inner critics. Raz thinks my outcomes are already fixed based on who I am and the habits I've formed until this point. She is just so narrow-minded.

Chantel Prat advises people to explore a growth mindset, but with caution. "While I'm all for a growth mindset, I also think many of us would be better off if we could stop to understand and embrace the way our brains work," she said. "There's a reason they do the things they do even if they drive us nuts in the process."[4]

As you can rewire your brain with experiences, you can consciously work to change your mindset. It's also understandable that many people will have a fixed mindset in certain areas and a growth mindset in others. My favorite word that helps people shift from a fixed mindset to a growth mindset is *yet*. I'm not an athlete *yet*. I'm not good at coding *yet*. I haven't scaled my business *yet*.

The growth mindset is a key tool during a setback to help you unlock your next move. Our brains are always changing. Humans are always evolving. We have the power to apply a growth mindset at any point in our lives, at any age, whether we're a barging baby or an apprehensive adult.

Seeing Ourselves through the Fragile Perception of Others

A study done by creativity researchers revealed that the number-one ingredient in creative achievement was "perseverance and resilience produced by the growth mindset....the love of challenge, belief in effort, resilience in the face of setbacks."[5]

The side effects of a growth mindset are truly fantastic. It even helps with self-esteem and confidence.

"The growth mindset lets people—even those who are targets of negative labels—use and develop their mind fully," Dweck says. "Their heads are not filled with limiting thoughts, a fragile sense of belonging and a belief that other people can define them."[6]

A fragile sense of belonging was something beauty and wellness influencer Cyrus Veyssi had to combat as a young, gender-nonconforming queer person growing up in the suburbs of Boston. Veyssi recalls how they didn't always have the words to describe their identity. "I was so insecure. I experienced gender dysphoria," they said. "At one point I remember trying on my mom's clothes and wondering if I was trans. All I ever heard was you're either a woman or a man, and if you transition your life will be so hard."

Veyssi had to work hard through their teenage years to embrace their true identity. Since then, they have modeled how to work through setback after setback, adopting a growth mindset, not just for themselves but for others in their orbit, and they have done so in a public forum.

So many of the stories in this book are about major moments that lead to life, career, or business setbacks. But Veyssi's story is one that demonstrates how impactful those daily microsetbacks can be, especially for those with a public persona. Their creative and thoughtful responses to the daily interactions they have with folks who can't, or don't want to, understand or respect their gender identity is one of the many things that make Veyssi such an inspiration.

"I think with each setback you become a bit more armed and a bit more equipped to work through the next one," they said as we chatted over Zoom one Friday afternoon. "Marginalized people deal with more setbacks. We've made a lot of progress but we have a lot more work to do. Part of my goal is to aid in that progress."

Can you think of a better example of someone who fully exemplifies a growth mindset?

Veyssi has a unique ability to weave together words, something that has served them well in their various career roles, from marketing strategist to content creator. In their early twenties, they drew on that creativity by making funny videos and posting them to TikTok and Instagram, which is what ultimately led to their rise as a social media celebrity.

"If the pandemic offered anything in my life it was the opportunity to take advantage of time," they said.

Like many young adults, Veyssi had moved back in with their parents during this period. As they spent more time with their family on a daily basis, they encountered many awkward yet loving moments.

That's what gave Veyssi the idea to create a video series that set their love of skincare, clothing and makeup against the backdrop of a loving, multigenerational family unexpectedly living together again under one roof. And while they were at it, they chose to demonstrate what a supportive relationship looks like between a straight Iranian father and his nonbinary, queer adult child. It was comedic, sweet, and authentic.

The first series to go viral was one that Veyssi posted of their dad—their baba, grilling in their yard. "I filmed myself saying something about how good my cocktail was, and then panned to my dad who was trying to teach me something about barbecuing," they said, laughing about how they had absolutely no interest in learning how to grill. "We were on such different pages. It was a true moment of a Millennial/Gen Z kid and their Boomer dad trying to connect. I labeled it 'My Straight Dad' and it got two to three million views the first week I posted it."

Making videos about two generations connecting over not connecting turned out to be Veyssi's sweet spot. They began to have more and more fun with their family, documenting their experiences together: shopping for makeup and skincare products with their dad, watching sports with their straight brother, and more, always finding creative and hilarious ways to demonstrate the sometimes uncomfortable yet always loving dynamic between themself and their straight male family members.

Veyssi and I met while working together at the same marketing firm. They started as an intern right out of college and worked their way up to a senior role as their fame skyrocketed. Now they are recognized by fans as they walk down the streets of New York City.

But Veyssi's rise in visibility also meant a rise in backlash.

By 2022, hints of progress had been made in terms of raising awareness and protecting against discrimination toward the nonbinary and transgender communities. That year, the U.S. State Department expanded the number of gender options citizens were able to check on their passport, beyond just "male" and "female." The U.S. Justice Department also sent a letter to all state attorneys, reinforcing the, "federal constitutional and statutory provisions that protect transgender youth against discrimination, including when those youth seek gender-affirming care."[7]

But the safety of these communities became a highly politicized debate in 2023 as states like Texas and Florida put complete bans on gender-affirming healthcare for minors. *The Texas Tribune* pointed out the devastating impacts this state law would have on young people, stating, "Trans kids, their parents and major medical groups say these medical treatments are important to protecting the mental health of an already vulnerable population, which faces a higher risk of depression and suicide than their cisgender peers."[8]

The protections at the federal level could go only so far to prevent state governments from enacting laws to undo those protections. Nor could they prevent the ongoing stigma, bullying, and hate that people who don't conform to traditional gender norms continue to face.

Nonconformity in any, well, form, could be considered a setback, or at least an obstacle. Those who do not conform to long upheld societal expectations are likely to experience more setbacks than those who do.

The backlash was difficult for Veyssi to endure. Some comments were merely an eye roll or vomit emoji, while others were violent and harmful, creating an impact not only on Veyssi themself but on the larger nonbinary, queer, and transgender communities who witnessed this public discourse unfolding across social media. Veyssi began to wonder if they should stop sharing so much. Despite all the work it took to get to this point, despite the wildly supportive community they had amassed, despite quitting that full time marketing job to go all in on becoming a content creator, Veyssi wondered if perhaps it was time to retreat from the spotlight.

"I used to be really angry at hateful comments," Veyssi admitted. "They always deeply impacted me, meaning if enough people commented negative things on a photo, I would take the photo down."

As they slipped into a setback, they fell into rumination and a spiral of self-consciousness.

When one user posed an extremely violent question that made Veyssi concerned for their own safety, they made the surprising decision not to retreat, but to reshare the comment. They amplified it publicly to their hundreds of thousands of followers, tagging the original commenter. Perhaps showing the hate would draw attention to the extent and severity of the bullying. Less than an hour later, so many people had rushed to Veyssi's defense, the original commenter had not only deleted the original spiteful comment, they had completely deactivated their account. Perhaps Veyssi was onto something with this new technique. Perhaps the love and support could drown out the hate.

Posting the hate publicly seemed to disarm it. With this insight, Veyssi started to tiptoe out of their setback. They continued to share humorous photos and videos—this time, without shame. Without fear.

Blame and Shame

As we've learned, some blame others when facing a setback; some blame themselves. It's often easier to protect our own egos by blaming others. People tend to fall along the spectrum of thinking a situation is all their fault or completely someone else's fault. The answer often lies in between.

"I often have to counsel people outside of thinking something was all their fault," Dr. Casarella said. "Situations usually come down to a dynamic. It's often not malicious. Most people are not all good or all bad."

Cyrus Veyssi could have blamed everyone else for their backlash—and they would have had every right to. But they applied a growth mindset to help them understand why people react the way they do in certain situations. They grew to see that showing compassion might actually be more effective than rumination, fear, or anger. It can be so easy to find someone to direct your anger at. To place blame. Good people do bad things. Bad people do terrible things. Well-intentioned people can exert behaviors that leave a terrible impact on others. A setback is rarely the fault of one person.

"Blaming ourselves often makes us weaker,"[9] Adam Grant said. "It leaves our confidence shattered. Blaming others makes us weaker, too. It prevents us from learning from our own mistakes."

"If you punish people for being wrong, they cover up their mistakes. They make excuses and throw blame to justify the past," Grant continued. "If you treat being wrong as a learning opportunity, people admit their errors. They take responsibility for correcting and preventing them in the future."[10]

He encourages us to accept that in most situations, it's not you, but it's also not me. It's us.

Therapists often say there are three entities in a relationship—person one, person two, and the relationship itself. And situations are rarely ever black and white. The answer lies within the gray.

Clean Out Your Junk Drawer

"It's important to realize what your triggers are and why you have default reactions to things," Dr. Casarella said. "But also what are these bigger societal messages? I always ask my clients, 'Where is this message coming from?' The message you received when you came back from maternity leave and were so self-conscious about proving your value—have you received the message that you aren't 'valuable' in other ways? Have you been cast aside or pushed down mountains you've climbed before?"

The way this woman can pull things out of my brain that I never could have on my own. And I'm the one living with this brain.

"Some thoughts are just junk drawer thoughts," she continued. "We don't realize all this crap is still clunking around in there because we never take the time to clean it out. We think we need to hold onto this and it continues to be our trigger."

Wait, is this why we lie awake at night reviewing random conversations and interactions from as far back as junior high? And replaying the experience in ways where our current self would have our former self reacting and responding very differently? Am I the only one who does this?

"Though it can feel like gaslighting when someone has a different reality from yours, it's also entirely possible that you both are reporting your version of the truth," said Chantel Prat. "At the end of the day, the way people remember a story reflects differences in the way they experienced the original event. The scientific explanation for this boils down to differences in perspective."[11]

As a neuroscientist, Prat understands a little bit (okay, a boatload more) about why our brains work like this. She says that when we remember an embarrassing or painful event, on some level we end up re-experiencing some of the emotions associated with the original event. We relive our pain and embarrassment over and over.

"It might make you blush or tear up," she said. "This is because the process of retrieving a stored memory places your brain into a state that strongly resembles the one it was in when the memory was originally recorded. Your brain counts this re-experiencing of the memory as a second learning event."

But our brains alter the memories. They shapeshift as we re-experience them.

"Re-experiencing the original memory both changes its nature and increases the likelihood that the event will be retrievable in the future," Prat said. "Memories, and even completely imagined events, can create learning effects that are similar to those created when your brain processes the information in real life."[12]

This is why setbacks are so critical to our self-development. We replay defining moments in our brains over and over again (at the risk of rumination and even obsession) because our subconscious minds are trying to learn from them. But our brains are also warping those memories. That's why it's so easy to review a negative memory, or a moment that brings up strong feelings, and when we see someone else in it, we direct our blame their way. Or we replay it and think about what we'd do differently. We shame ourselves for not reacting "better."

At the risk of sounding obvious, we need to be kinder to ourselves, and to others. "Most people would not expect a five-year-old to immediately know how to tie their shoes," Dr. Casarella said. "If they can't do it right away we send them the message that they are learning and they can keep trying. You know they're going to tie it wrong the first time. Why don't we treat ourselves like that?"

"You're never 'doing it wrong,' you're learning," said Dr. Casarella. "That's what the Setback Cycle is—a season of learning."

When a Growth Mindset Fosters Personal Evolution

Drawing on the support of those around them, Cyrus Veyssi was able to slowly emerge, adopting a growth mindset to finally recognize that any hateful comments directed their way were not at all about them. After all, these people didn't actually know Veyssi; they just saw a person in a video on a tiny two-dimensional screen. This personal growth has led them to process the often anonymous backlash much more quickly.

As one user commented, "Give it up, you'll never be a girl, bro," another wrote, "You are a he/him no matter what you think." Veyssi responded to the latter with, "Hi friend. I'm so sorry you're feeling sad and projecting your feelings on the internet. It's painful—and the hardest part is that it's not effective. Tough to hear, I know! See, you can call me or think of me however you want. And at the end of the day, I'll live my life free and joyous and proud of who I am. I hope one day you'll experience that feeling and find out what's causing you so much pain. An open heart is worth so much more than a closed mind."

"Anybody trying to identify your traumas is just unveiling their own," they explained during our conversation. Veyssi reframed how they thought about the criticism and decided to use it as an opportunity. They now frequently respond to hate with love.

I admired how Veyssi tackled their trolls not by blaming them or even ignoring them, but by acknowledging them and embracing them, and in doing so, making them powerless. It's almost as if Veyssi thought more highly of the haters than the haters did of themselves.

It took a lot of rewiring and untraining for Veyssi to be able to address these situations with the level of grace they do now. Now I realize they are absolute proof that adopting a growth mindset can unlock creativity.

The beauty industry began to recognize the value Veyssi was offering, and within a year of posting these fun family videos, they were approached for campaigns with brands like NARS, Rare Beauty, Marc Jacobs and more.

Veyssi is now a coveted beauty influencer and is frequently flown around the world to participate in campaigns for top brands. They continue to post a blend of beauty and makeup videos, alongside the more comical family videos.

They also continue to be an outspoken advocate for queer and nonbinary communities. Veyssi credits their ability to do this with the support of their incredibly loving friends and family. And yet they recognize that not every family offers the type of support that theirs does.

"I feel like it's a double-edged sword," they said. "On the one hand, I think it's really exciting, important and inspiring to see a relationship between this Middle Eastern hetero-masculine man and his unapologetic acceptance of his queer, nonbinary kid, which we rarely see. My purpose has been to debunk all of the comments from strangers who see my content and assume that I must be estranged from my family or that my family doesn't accept me."

"On the other hand, I think it could potentially be harmful to show this type of relationship," they pointed out. "I worry about not acknowledging that the relationship between a lot of queer people and their parents isn't this way. This isn't the norm. So I don't want people to come to my page, see my relationship with my parents and be like, see how far we've come?"

One of the things that drew me to Veyssi's videos was the thoughtfulness, adaptability, eagerness to learn and grow and to bring others along on that journey—including their extra cooperative, often hilarious baba. They are expertly able to turn the script around and show that close family dynamic, even when it's unexpected.

"I've never wanted to be the poster child for representation between straight and queer communities because I think it's so multifaceted," they said. "It's important for people to see that acceptance, unapologetic, unconditional love should be the norm. I get a lot of messages from people who don't have relationships with their parents thanking me for creating this content because they feel like they've found a safe space. I want them to know this shouldn't be a privilege, it should be the bare minimum."

Veyssi is still working to update that narrative every day, bringing more support and sharing that unconditional love with their millions of fans around the world. Even the haters.

Cyrus Veyssi Setback Cycle Snapshot

Phase 1: ESTABLISH	Veyssi began filming funny videos of their sweet, loving, and sometimes awkward interactions with the rest of their family, which, because of their gender nonconformity, led to bullying and online hate. This triggered the memory of being teased as a young child. Veyssi took down some of their posts and hid for a bit.
Phase 2: EMBRACE	Veyssi questioned whether to continue being so public on social media and paused to consider why the often anonymous criticism bothered them so much. During their thaw out, Veyssi's growth mindset enabled them to come to the realization that most people were simply projecting their own insecurities and expectations of what those born as a certain gender should act like, look like, dress like, and more. Veyssi reframed how they thought about the criticisms, and decided to use how they responded as an opportunity to demonstrate compassion and honesty.
Phase 3: EXPLORE	Veyssi stopped taking the insults personally. As they began to share more about their loving family with confidence and grace, the attention and support poured in. They garnered hundreds of thousands of fans on TikTok and Instagram, and the love began to overpower the hate.
Phase 4: EMERGE	They reached new levels of fame, appearing often as the first nonbinary model in makeup and skincare campaigns. They hope to reach kids who, like their childhood self, are still struggling to figure out their identity. They continue to explore more ways to advocate for inclusion, showing what can happen when one chooses to celebrate their identity rather than hide it.

Letting Go of Embrace

The Embrace phase can be a blip for some, and endless for others. The S curve of the Setback Cycle can be long and windy, arching and dipping as you find your footing. For others, it can be a short swerve or a never-ending stretch. No matter how you got through Embrace, my hope is that after working through it, you'll feel a release from whatever was holding you back. You have gotten to know your inner critic and can exist alongside it. You know how to turn up the volume on your hype person. You've embraced the fact that a behavior does not define your identity. You know how to adjust your expectations now that you understand their origins. You can adopt a growth mindset, even when you feel personally attacked, because you also have a better understanding of how blame and shame can be tricky tools that hinder progress.

You're energized and motivated to find a new path. You're ready to make the necessary decisions that will allow you to move forward.

You're starting to get curious about what more might be possible.

PHASE 3
EXPLORE

CHAPTER 5

Cultivate Your Curiosity

Know that thing you've been meaning to try one day? "One day" has arrived.

We dipped a toe into our curiosity a bit during Embrace, but in Explore we'll fully dive in. There are the daily curiosities in the articles we read, the quick facts we look up, and the conversations we have with those around us that shape how we see the world. Then there's Curiosity with a capital C. You have to excavate a bit to get to that one. These are the things you've always wondered about, those dreams buried within you that haven't been unlocked or acknowledged in a long time—maybe ever. The roots of your Curiosity can be found in the form of hobbies you loved as a kid, or fantasies you once had but pushed down because they felt too frivolous, and you felt it would be too selfish to incorporate them into your life so you tucked them neatly away in a dresser. Well, it's time to open the drawer.

The aftermath of a setback is a great time for exploring our deep-rooted Curiosities and bringing them to the surface.

Once you recognize that certain goals you once strived for no longer hold value, it's time to redefine what success looks like. It's stopping to ask, *Is this really serving me? Is this all I have to offer the world? Am I okay with just fine or am I simply afraid to move on?* It's okay to continue. It's also okay to acknowledge that it might be time to walk away from the journey you've been on. To say, *Maybe this wasn't it after all.*

Anytime you hit a fork in the road, Curiosity offers a broader understanding of what might be possible.

What would you do if you weren't afraid? Of course we all have responsibilities—to ourselves, to our families, to each other. We have rent, perhaps even mortgages to pay. Meanwhile, we've been conditioned to think of things like indulging in hobbies or activities that don't directly result in financial gain or benefit society in some way as a frivolous waste of time. But start to daydream for a moment. How would you spend your days if money were no issue? Is there a way you could incorporate a tiny drop of that into your actual daily life? If so, what could that look like? Reading more, playing sports, doodling, writing, playing the piano, knitting, crafting? There's a reason adult coloring books exist.

Scientists cite Curiosity (the big one) and the act of learning new skills as the key to longevity.[1] A study from 1996 confirmed that curiosity helps maintain central nervous system health. Another study from Harvard in 2018 demonstrated the organizational benefits of encouraging employees at large corporations to explore their curiosity in meaningful ways.[2] Simple activities to foster curiosity (little C is good for you, too!) exploration like reading, taking a walk and turning off your Google maps so you can get lost and find your way back, doing crossword puzzles, and more can go far to keep one's brain sharp. Novelty and discovery are important no matter how old we get. In fact, they become even more critical to well-being as we age.

The possibility of moving out of your rut *and* living longer? Seems like it might be worth the effort. So how do you turn the volume up on that Curiosity so you can truly tune into what you're craving?

The Curiosity Quiz

Get to Know Idealist You

Think back to your childhood, or your early, idealistic years, whenever those years may have been.

- What are you doing when you feel most like yourself?
- Where do you retreat when you want to escape or relax?
- What's the one hobby you've always enjoyed above everything else, or the one thing in life you've loved since you were little?
- What did you enjoy doing as a kid? Did you play an instrument? Do team sports? Read under a tree?
- What was exciting and fun about doing those activities? What did you love about them?

If you struggled with this, that's fine. It's important to look beyond childhood—after all, childhood wasn't idealistic for all of us. Plus, our interests evolve over time. Angela Duckworth, psychologist and author of *Grit*, suggests asking those around you what you're interested in. That's right: the people who know and love you might be able to tell you what lights you up. Sometimes they can see you more clearly than you see yourself.

Whether you're taking it alone or have enlisted a friend or loved one to collaborate, continue with the Curiosity quiz, blending the fun stuff into your daily routines.

Introduce Idealist You to Realist You

- Who are you now? Don't say what your job is—in one sentence, write down who you are as a person. How would your best friend describe you?
- If you stare out the window for five minutes and let your mind wander, where does it go? If you haven't allowed yourself to daydream in a while, go ahead. Where do those dreams take you?
- If money weren't a factor and you could have any job you wanted, what would you do?
- What is fear preventing you from doing?
- How could you take one small baby step toward doing that thing you're afraid of?

If you're heading into the default excuse, "I don't have the time or energy for exploring this Curiosity; I'm just trying to get by day to day," trust me, I understand. A lot of people struggle with this. I struggled with it and I'm the one who wrote it. But is it really time or energy that worries you? Or is it that nagging fear about where your Curiosity might lead you?

That inner critic can be a real barrier to exploration. Curiosity is in constant battle with it. The inner critic can be Curiosity's Achilles' heel. Our damn inner critic tends to point us toward the things that offer immediate satisfaction. Figuring out your deep rooted Curiosity takes time, effort and a learning curve. We often ignore the discomfort and patience required to dig deep and figure out what we might want to change. It's the same discomfort we try to avoid by not acknowledging our emotions. We try so hard to ignore it, we pretend it isn't there.

In fact, our inner critic has infiltrated so many parts of our lives that people, especially women, have been conditioned to ignore their own physical pain. That pain is also, unfortunately, ignored in many medical settings. According to the *Journal of the American Heart Association*, women who visited emergency departments with chest pain in 2022 waited 29 percent longer than men to be evaluated for possible heart attacks.[3] Even worse, a National Institute of Health–funded study suggests that middle-aged women are twice as likely as middle-aged men to be diagnosed with a mental illness if their symptoms are consistent with heart disease.[4] It makes sense—being told by medical professionals that nothing is wrong when you're experiencing symptoms and know your own body is "off" can understandably drive someone crazy.

The act of ignoring our discomfort, be it mental, physical, or both, is certain to have a detrimental impact on our health.

Lights, Camera, Identity Crisis

Reality TV star and fashion icon Stacy London was taken aback as she entered her late forties. From jobs at high-end fashion magazines like *Vogue* and *Mademoiselle* to Pantene spokesperson to her extraordinarily long tenure hosting TLC's acclaimed reality show, *What Not to Wear*, London spent more than a decade defining fashion and style, beloved by audiences for her authority and candor on the subject.

Yet around 2017, London started to observe a shift. She recalls how at age forty-six, she was no longer being asked to do campaigns across the fashion industry where she was once heralded as a style icon. She even went back to her TV roots. "I tried to pitch a show about middle age and transformation and multigenerational mentorship," she said. "And people told me that it wasn't cool. It didn't seem like a sexy idea."

London cycled through a myriad of emotions during this time. She struggled to get herself out of her rut. Her entire identity had been shaken. "If I'm not that girl from *What Not to Wear*, who am I?" she asked herself. This wasn't London's first setback. She recalled a time when she was fired from her job as the editor of a high-end fashion magazine at the age of twenty-six.

"Being fired was the best thing that happened to me," she said during our interview, more than twenty-five years later.

London certainly didn't feel that way while she was going through the experience. Her inner critic was screaming at her upon her firing, worrying that she didn't have enough talent to get another job, that her career was over. She looks back and realizes that this moment was her turning point. After being fired, she took on jobs as a personal stylist which is when she started styling people of all different sizes, not just the homogenous-looking models she had previously styled in '90s fashion magazine photo shoots. It's what led her to the insight that when people feel good in their clothing, it significantly impacts their self-esteem. That insight is what eventually landed her the role as host of TLC's *What Not to Wear*, a show that lasted for more than a decade.

"If I hadn't been able to dress real people, if I'd only ever been able to dress models," she said in an article she wrote for *Fast Company*, "I would never have been qualified for that position."[5]

Fast-forward to her late forties, as she was surprised, humiliated, and also confused about how suddenly this entertainment industry and overall societal rejection seemed to arrive. She felt, as many women her age do, relevant, energetic, even rebelliously stylish. Why weren't these TV producers seeing that? Society's perception of the over-forty woman didn't match London's own experience. Surrounded by a vast network of peers who were doing amazing things from running companies to working on initiatives that would not only yield significant profits but literally change the world—why was no one trying to engage what she knew was a huge audience with high spending potential? It seemed like such a missed opportunity.

The Rejection Reflection

Neuroscientists have found that the feeling of rejection can actually cause physical pain. "Your brain lights up in ways that are similar to processing physical pain," said Adam Grant.[6] "You can see the same physiological response when people who have recently been dumped are shown pictures of their exes."

"Rejection hurts," he said. "You can't just ignore it."

Do you know how much rejection entrepreneurs trying to put a new idea into the world have to endure? There's a reason most founders feel like swans gliding along a lake. They appear to float effortlessly and gracefully while frantically paddling below the surface, trying desperately to stay above water.

"Rejection hurts because it threatens our identity," Grant continued. "That's especially true if you see your work as a reflection of who you are.... The mistake we often make is putting all our eggs in one identity basket. Because the reality is, we all have multiple identities. Psychologists have found that this can be a source of resilience. When one identity is threatened, we can lean on a different identity."[7]

Stacy London did exactly this. When she faced rejection from the fashion world, she leaned on her other identities—the reliable friend, the ultimate hypewoman, an inherently creative person who wanted to find new ways to help people through tough situations. That's what eventually led her to her next chapter.

As she dealt with confusion, annoyance, and anger over her career rejection, London was dealt another blow as she mourned the loss of her father, who she had been very close with. After he passed away, she started experiencing a slew of perplexing symptoms—dry skin, heart palpitations, joint pain, insomnia, night sweats, and temperature fluctuation. London attributed it to grief at first. Eventually she sought counsel from the medical community, going from doctor to doctor yet finding little by way of answers, let alone solutions. It was the classic battle of curiosity versus the inner critic, but this time her physical health was at risk. She was playing a very unfun game of "Is it them? Is it me? Is it them?" and so on.

As the symptoms grew worse, she followed her Curiosity by frantically researching cures for her strange symptoms, exploring natural remedies, mindfulness, anything that might work. She also knew there was power in taking a pause, so she prioritized rest as much as she could. Eventually, she came to a startling conclusion that, in retrospect, perhaps should have been obvious: she was in perimenopause.

London wasn't alone. Despite the fact that 85 percent of women experience menopausal symptoms, she couldn't find many resources offering practical solutions to these very common problems.[8] "There aren't a lot of doctors who really understand that menopause needs to be treated not as a disease, but as a natural phase that comes with impacts and effects that make you feel differently," she said. "Plus, every symptom of menopause can be explained away or attributed to something else."

Menopausal or not, how many times have we ignored our symptoms or rationalized them away?

Meanwhile, it turns out medical students study menopause for only two hours over the course of their many years of schooling.[9] London was shocked to find the lack of resources or solutions to mitigate some of the more unpleasant symptoms of menopause (which, as a reminder, is a natural, biological issue that impacts half the population!)

Twelve percent of the Earth's population will be menopausal by 2025.[10] "Doctors classify it as a disease, but it's not a disease, it's a physiological transition we have to learn to manage," London said. "If we're going to live to be eighty, ninety, one hundred, lots of us will spend one-third of our lives in menopause."

"When I really started to see how many things are really surrounding this, you see the sexism, misogyny, the ageism, and then we don't talk about the underserved communities, people of color, the LGBT community, who are really struggling with these symptoms," she said. But rather than ruminate in blaming society for ignoring or gaslighting people going through menopause, London wanted to figure out a way to address it. The realization she was forming was that one person's crisis might end up benefiting an entire generation.

Redefining Midlife

London was in an FFT, which she says lasted about four years before she realized what was happening. She spent that time working through her "oh, fuck" moment by diving into research around, well, the lack of research, resources, and information around menopause, which she found astounding considering the amount of people impacted by this natural phase of life.

Rather than disappear into oblivion, as society (and several TV producers) seemed to think she should, London sought out people who were willing to have more candid conversations about their collective experience. She worked her way through the Embrace phase, reframing difficulties as opportunities as she tried to get those around her to open up the conversation about aging in general. It wasn't just the loss of earning potential, the physical and emotional changes, and the general devaluing of women as they reach a certain age, it was also the fact that nobody seemed to be out there talking about it.

She continued down her Curiosity rabbit hole. Instead of Alice in Wonderland, she was Stacy in midlife. She asked around and found a few communities that did, in fact, focus on this demographic. Margit Detweiler's TueNight, a private community of forty- to sixty-plus women, offers events, workshops, and a private community called the TueNighters where members share the hilarious, often messy, and too real stories of what happens in their now "grown-ass lives." She connected with these women and many others, noting that the work they were doing was not only brilliant, it was (sadly) revolutionary.

As London worked her way out of Embrace and into Explore, she reflected on how much her own self-esteem issues had impacted her career choices throughout her entire life. It was the light bulb moment that allowed her to unlock that deep-rooted Curiosity.

"I got into the menopause industry for the same reason I got into fashion—insecurity," she said. "Since I was a child I had a rash all over my body because of psoriasis. I felt ugly. I had such low self-esteem, so I went into fashion, an industry that feeds off of people with low self-esteem. I wanted to make other people feel better about themselves, but I was also trying to find a way to feel better about myself."

Through some of her new connections, she was introduced to an emerging personal care company called State of Menopause, which included products that alleviated the symptoms of menopause. Going all in on her newfound mission, London acquired the company, taking the reins as their CEO. One of her first acts in that role was to eliminate the word "women" from the website so it could be more gender inclusive. After all, it's not just women who experience menopause.

London also pointed out that so many opportunities will be overlooked if we continue to ignore middle age. "Midlife is a life phase ripe with opportunity and we are not taking it," she said. "Menopause is nature's fail-safe to force you to focus on your body. Before then, biology and society dictate that you are meant to care for others. Now that's done, so go focus on yourself. Make your side hustle into a billion-dollar business. Travel to all the places you have always wanted to see."

Thanks to founders like London, the bullshit promise of positive psychology has given way to radical transparency and new ways of defining success.

Perhaps some core part of your identity has been challenged during a setback, and as London did, you can't help but rethink everything that has led to this. Yes, this sucks—there is no getting around that. But in the reflection, can you find patterns? Once London was able to process what was happening to her, emotionally and physically, she was able to trust her own instincts and lean into her Curiosity to come up with solutions. She paid attention to what her gut knew to be true, even when well-respected doctors told her, "Just deal with it."

London was finally Emerging from her setback as she took on this new role. She stayed on as CEO for about eighteen months. During that time, hot flashes became a hot topic as menopause was starting to dominate the zeitgeist. London seized this moment, organizing the first ever Menopause CEO summit. Suddenly everyone realized this enormity of the demographic looking for solutions to a rarely discussed issue, and this group had money to spend. The *New York Times* published an article titled, "Welcome to the Menopause Gold Rush."

Soon celebrities started paying attention, creating their own companies to hop on the bandwagon. Naomi Watts created Stripes, selling beauty products that targeted those experiencing menopausal symptoms, Drew Barrymore opened up about having a hot flash on her national talk show. Even Goop and Gwyneth Paltrow started getting involved in the conversation, selling multivitamins specifically designed for this demographic. London is thrilled that the menopause industry is gaining such momentum and that these big names are continuing the work to help destigmatize the topic. She hopes the movement will prompt more research and the development of practical solutions to make this phase of life more manageable for those who eventually experience it. London is proud of her contributions in pushing that movement[11] forward.

"There are a lot of people who would like to keep me in a fashion and style box because that's what I've done for twenty years," she said. "But my own existential crisis with perimenopause brought me to this. I really started to think about the fact that I have spent my life telling people, if you look better, you're going to feel better. At a certain point in my journey, and maybe because of my age, I care less about style and more about health. If you feel better, you're going to look better instead of the other way around. I'm simply doing what I've always done."

Remember her idea for that reality show about midlife? She didn't give up after those Hollywood executives told her no. Pinterest TV picked it up as one of their initial content offerings. And ten years after the show ended its run, London reunited with her *What Not To Wear* co-host, Clinton Kelly, to create *The Stacy & Clinton Show*, a ten-city live tour across the country.

London's crisis led her to double down on her Curiosity, which paved the way for her to identify her true purpose. And it went well beyond fashion and style.

Stacy London Setback Cycle Snapshot

Phase 1: ESTABLISH	After years as a lauded fashion icon and TV star, London faced overwhelming rejection in the same places where she'd always found support. At the same time, she experienced confusing physical symptoms while caring for her sick father.
Phase 2: EMBRACE	As she processed the overwhelming grief and pain over her father's death, she got caught in the rumination trap and experienced a freeze. Doctor after doctor told her nothing was wrong. London's intuition, and her body, told her otherwise. She did some research to arrive at what should have been an obvious diagnosis from a medical professional—she was in perimenopause. Applying a growth mindset, London began to think about how to reframe the difficulties she was experiencing as an opportunity.
Phase 3: EXPLORE	London allowed herself to go deep into her Curiosity as she started having public conversations about menopause and middle age in a way that began to bring these topics to cultural prominence. No stranger to setbacks, London also started to wonder what she could do next if her TV career was truly on pause. Part of her identity was helping people feel good about themselves. London explored how she might do that now by boosting people's self-esteem through solving the lack of candor and education around menopause.
Phase 4: EMERGE	With clear vision and a consistent mission, London took the reins and is looking to change the narrative and experience of women in midlife. In a glorious full-circle moment, her show about midlife and menopause was picked up by Pinterest TV.

Upon hearing London's story, Shoshanna Hecht reflected, "It's a really good example of doubling down on strengths and purpose."

It's true. Stacy London has always known, deep down, that her purpose is to be the ultimate hype person, a role she proudly wears, even today. She did that originally through the lens of style and helping people boost their self-esteem by wearing clothing that honored their personal style, and later through demystifying the conversation around menopause, showing the world how those in midlife can be, and deserve to be, celebrated.

Dopamine Dips and Rewards-Based Learning

Chantel Prat does not think we should necessarily explore *all* of our curiosity without boundaries. "There is some really fascinating research around curiosity," she told me. "But curiosity is not always a good thing. When you find yourself in an unknown situation there might be danger. There might be goodies and all kinds of wonderful things to learn that will guide you and change you. But what happens when predictions go wrong? Why are we curious? What facts do we need in order to make decisions?"

I suppose that by trade, neuroscientists are expected to be incredibly thoughtful, yet Prat's level of thoughtfulness always seems to blow me away whenever I catch up with her.

Be open to learning, acknowledge what Curiosity might be available for exploration, approach things with a growth mindset, but always trust your intuition.

Prat told me that the brain makes decisions by trying to maximize rewards and minimize punishment. It uses past experiences and decisions to predict what you should do next. Our own personal playbooks are informed by previously stored information, as well as intuition.

Perhaps logic versus intuition isn't necessarily a battle. Decisions are best made and Curiosity best explored when those two work together.

"Your brain finds intellectual engagement and taking in new information rewarding," Prat said. "Compliments, great food, sex, anything that you find rewarding results in dopamine being released in the brain."

When things start going really well, our brains receive a signal that basically says we are winning at life. But as we see more and more success, we need even more dopamine to maintain that level of excitement and happiness. The standards, and the stakes, get higher. So how do we evaluate success and manage our dopamine response based on these new, higher standards?

The ideal situation is achieved when we connect the dots between what we want to create, where we want to go, and weave in what we're really good at. It's time to talk about our superpowers.

CHAPTER 6

From Superpower to Purpose

Establish sets us up to work through the Setback Cycle. Embrace encourages us to reflect, allow ourselves to process our feelings and adopt a growth mindset. Explore inspires us to ask, *What did I learn? What can I do? What do I want to do?* as we connect, catalyze, and consider our choices.

A fun way to find the answer to "What *can* I do?" is to figure out what our superpowers are.

"How do you take your special sauce and capture it in a way that can be applicable to something new?" Shoshanna Hecht asked. "In the business world these are called transferable skills. What that really means is, how do you take your gifts and harness them so you can do something that lights you up, that isn't just the grind, that isn't just you floating along?"

Talent is just a starting point. Hard work beats lazy talent.
—ROBIN ARZÓN

One might be inclined to define their "superpower" as talent. What have people praised you for throughout your life? What comes naturally to you? But also, what do you love doing? Your innate superpower is more than just talent or something you do with ease. Can you think of a combination of what you're good at and what you love? Can you reframe the idea that you aren't good at something *yet*? Remember, a growth mindset allows us to improve in any area. Passion + skill + motivation to practice and improve at that skill = your superpowers.

This concept reminds me of the movie *A League of Their Own*, where two sisters join the All-American Girls Professional Baseball League. Dottie and Kit both play on the Rockford Peaches team. Dottie is lauded for her excellent baseball skills. Kit isn't nearly as good at it, but she absolutely loves it. For Kit, baseball is her purpose; it's what she wants to be doing. Dottie does it because she is like all of us; we do what we've been told we are skilled at. Her talents bring her there, but it's clearly not her passion.

Kit, on the other hand, loves baseball more than anything. That passion is what motivates her to work hard, practice, and improve. Kit's superpower isn't baseball, though. Being good at baseball is the result. Her superpower is drive and determination, which allows her to find success in the sport she loves so much.

"It's much easier to intuit what we love than to know what we're good at," added Chantel Prat, who has done significant research around aptitude in her lab.

"One of, if not the largest, predictor of success in any circumstance is motivation," Prat said. "Most things worth doing are hard. Most things we struggle with are hard, like computationally difficult. When the brain decides whether or not to attempt to learn a new thing, it's estimating whether or not this will be rewarding for you based on your values."

"I could bring you into the lab and tell you you're below average in language learning, but if you fall in love with someone who speaks French as their native language, suddenly your motivation for learning is going to send your aptitude through the roof," she continued. "Not because of how your brain works but because at the heart of this is motivation."

Motivation can compensate for a lack of natural talent. It's the thing that makes us apply grit to any given task. This is the basis for psychologist Angela Duckworth's Grit Theory, which says talent + effort = skill, but skill + effort = achievement. In other words, no matter how much talent one is born with, skill can be gained only through effort and practice. Achievement is what happens when one puts those acquired skills into continued practice—that's perseverance. The Grit Theory points out that those who persevere tend to succeed more than those who coast along because of some extraordinary natural ability.

"Motivation itself could be a superpower," Prat said. "You might not know what you're good at, but most people know what they like and don't like and that is a signal from your brain about what conditions it imagines to be rewarding for you."

The Rise of an Icon

Fashion legend Norma Kamali is best known for the sleeping bag coat, hotpants and the bold red bathing suit popularized by Farrah Fawcett, currently on display at the Smithsonian National Museum of American History in Washington, D.C. Throughout her remarkably long career, she has been no stranger to setbacks.

Kamali was born in Manhattan in 1945 to Lebanese and Basque parents.[1] Her father died when she was young so she was mostly raised by her mother, an artist. Kamali's interest in the arts began at a young age. She remembers sitting by the river and sketching as a child.

She earned a scholarship to the Fashion Institute of Technology, even though she hated fashion at the time. She couldn't stand the garter belts and the "matchy matchy" *Mad Men*–style designs of the early sixties. She was more drawn to secondhand stores that sold pieces from the 1940s, which is what Kamali frequently wore even though it was unconventional for that time. This was before vintage became chic.

Upon graduation, she took a job as a clerk at Northwest Orient Airlines. Kamali saw it as a way to travel the world. On her weekly trips to Paris and London, she was introduced to Europe's underground punk rock nightclubs. Kamali recalls the fashion across the Atlantic as drastically different from what she saw back home. She remembers the vibrant color "bursting, literally bursting."[2] She came back from London wearing a miniskirt and remembers cars screeching to a halt, thinking she was a prostitute. The audacity of showing your knees in the mid-1960s was, as Kamali put it, "Radical."

Inspired by the colorful and progressive styles she saw in London, she began creating her own clothes and selling them. She opened a shop on East 53rd Street called Kamali, paying just over $200 a month in rent. While still employed at the airline, she kept the store, and her entire clothing business, a secret from her colleagues. But she couldn't keep her superpower a secret for long. Eventually, her store caught the attention of some fashion magazines.

When *Time* magazine photographed Kamali for a story on snakeskin, a material she was among the first in the U.S. to use, her boss slapped down the magazine onto a desk in anger. They were not supportive of her side hustle. A few months later, Kamali left the airline and focused 100 percent on the clothing business.

Some of her earliest designs were among the boldest and most provocative the U.S. had ever seen. She made "hot pants" because she wanted to figure out how to make miniskirts even shorter, and the way to do that was to turn them into short shorts. (I'm not clear on why short shorts were named hot pants, but I like it and I think maybe they're back in style now?) Kamali put velvet appliques and designs on these spectacularly colorful, fun, patterned shorts. From snakeskin to hot pants, Kamali finally found a way to make clothing exciting. And it wasn't just her—people everywhere were craving a departure from the conservative, restricting styles of the '50s and early '60s. That was Kamali's absolute superpower—the way she could predict emerging cultural trends and get ahead of them before they took off.

In 1975, Kamali invented the sleeping bag coat, which was the birth of the entire puffer jacket industry. She loved camping, and one cold night she was trying to figure out how to get out of her sleeping bag to go to the bathroom in the woods. She took her sleeping bag with her and that's what gave her the idea to make it into a coat. "The first sleeping bag coat was my actual sleeping bag," she laughed.[3]

The sleeping bag coats were an instant hit. Once Studio 54 opened, the doormen wore them to keep warm while standing outside all night long. People started to think that if they wore sleeping bag coats in line for the club, that they might have a better chance of getting in. "I did not dissuade them," Kamali said with a smile in her voice.

"The 1970s started to be, especially in New York, an incredibly expressive time. There was such an energy," Kamali said. "It sort of was what London was in the 1960s."

As usual, Kamali was about a decade ahead of the trend.

Fashion shows were narrated at the time, and Bette Midler narrated Kamali's first show. Kamali remembers showing off some of her most outlandish designs like big-polka dot ruffle jackets, gold lamé capris, platform shoes—clothing and accessories nobody had seen before. Legendary New York Times style photographer Bill Cunningham was also there and happened to snap a ton of photos.

When I asked Kamali how she felt confident enough to ask Bette Midler to narrate the show and to get Bill Cunningham to take photos, she told me, "Well, you have to remember, Bette Midler wasn't Bette Midler yet. I wasn't Norma Kamali yet."

So how could someone this inventive, this bold, this ahead of the curve, with her incredible superpower to predict what people would want before they wanted it, a group of budding celebrity friends and a blooming fashion business, ever have a setback?

His name was Eddie. Norma met Eddie Kamali when she was only nineteen and they quickly married. He was a student studying economics, so he helped her manage the store. She recalled that his good looks and charm made him a successful salesperson. In fact, he was the one who pushed her to charge ten times more than what she originally thought her pieces were worth.

"I assumed, like everyone else, that men were better at business than women," Kamali said. So she let Eddie handle the finances.

Eddie was more extroverted than Kamali, so he would go out every night while she would stay back. It turned out, he was spending money from the store on his own social life.

There was infidelity, too, which didn't bother Kamali as much as the financial situation. But when he began dating a saleswoman from the store, their relationship reached a tipping point.

"There's always that one thing that happens that's so horrific," Kamali said, "that you thank your lucky stars it happened because you'll make the right move." One day, the saleswoman who was sleeping with her husband insisted that she, not Norma Kamali whose name was on the door, would be the new designer. The woman began instructing Kamali to make new designs. At that moment, as if on cue, the ceiling fell down over the store's back workstation.

If there was ever a sign to leave, this one could not be more clear. Her setback was Established.

Kamali had only ninety-eight dollars to her name. But when the ceiling, literally and figuratively, fell down, she walked away from the store. She felt it was the only way she could truly separate from her husband completely. She moved into an apartment with only a mattress and her clothes. She had given up everything she had worked for, had no money to show for it, and as she entered Embrace, she fell into a freeze, completely unsure of how to move forward.

But this was Norma Kamali, whose superpower had always enabled her to look ahead.

At one point, a reporter from the *Los Angeles Times* reached out to Kamali to do a story on her. During the interview, the reporter began to understand Kamali's financial situation, and asked her if there was anything she needed. Kamali knew exactly how to respond. She said bluntly and without pause, "I need everything."

The reporter ended up finding someone who could lend her a sewing machine. This was a growth mindset shift for the overly introverted Kamali. "I realized that if you talk to people and tell them what you need, something can happen," she said. She saw that there was no shame in asking for help. That's what enabled her to move into Explore, where she finally started making clothes once again.

Kamali's new business launched in 1978. She called it OMO, which stood for "On My Own." Eventually she found another space, which started as a sample room. She began to really explore her curiosity by working with sweatshirt fabric in designs, from swim cover-ups to jumpsuits, work suits and more, something that had never been done before. Kamali knew that someone could probably stand to make a lot of money on this innovation, and this time, it was going to be her.

Three years later, her brand had gone global and she was bringing in more than $11 million in business. Kamali Emerged gloriously from her setback.

Kamali has been tuning into her innate creativity ever since, even as she works her way through the inevitable swirls and dips and turns around various Setback Cycle S curves, big and small. Even in recent years, at the beginning of the pandemic, she once again did what she does best—tapped into what society was craving in the current moment. With everyone at home and spending more time there than ever before, Kamali stepped out of her usual luxury aesthetic and turned toward the comfort people were seeking in that moment, designing her own line of oversized home pillows.

Kamali continues to break barriers, innovate, and remain on top of cultural trends to this day. She's the one who designed Martha Stewart's bathing suit when Stewart posed at the age of eighty-one for her now iconic *Sports Illustrated* cover. And when the sport of pickleball rose to cultural consciousness seemingly out of nowhere, she sprang into action and came out with a pickleball dress. Who would have thought? The ingenuity and creativity of Norma Kamali know no bounds. Fifty years after those early trips to London, she continues to draw on the superpowers that made her a cultural icon.

Norma Kamali Setback Cycle Snapshot

Phase 1: ESTABLISH	The ceiling literally fell down over Kamali's workstation after she found out about her husband's infidelity and financial transgressions. She decided to walk away from him and the successful business they'd built.
Phase 2: EMBRACE	With only ninety-eight dollars to her name, she had given up everything she had worked for, had no money to show for it, and was at a loss of how to move forward. She certainly fell into rumination and a freeze before harnessing a growth mindset and letting go of blame and shame so she could move forward.
Phase 3: EXPLORE	With her past behind her, Kamali tapped into her unique trendspotting superpower and slowly started designing clothing again. Eventually, she built up enough of an inventory to launch her own business and open a new store—this time called OMO (on my own).
Phase 4: EMERGE	Kamali remains on the cusp of what's about to trend in culture to this day. She continues to defy fashion industry norms by boasting a fifty plus–year career. As a savvy Setback Cycler and trendsetter, she'll be able to handle whatever comes next.

So, What's Your Superpower?

There are a ton of articles, team building exercises, and TED Talks that offer to help you identify your superpower, mostly as it relates to the business world. Starting to unearth your superpowers can be done by answering a few simple questions:[4]

> **Identify Your Superpowers**
> - What have people told you you're amazing at?
> - What feels effortless to you that others struggle with?
> - What do people learn when they first meet you?
> - What do you see more clearly than others?
> - What do people say when they brag about you?
> - In a work setting, what would fall apart if you were to leave?

As with the Curiosity Quiz, sometimes those around you can identify your superpower more easily than you can. You may not realize you're a superhero, but they do.

Doing Good and Having Fun

I discovered one of my superpowers in my own neighborhood.

I absolutely love Sunnyside, Queens—the one hundred-year-old London plane trees that create leafy arches over the streets, the fact that we're only a fifteen-minute subway ride to midtown Manhattan, the baristas who have been greeting my daughter every day since she was an infant, the local yoga studio owner who is also a community activist, the vintage store owner who tells kids, "Everyone could use a little magic." I mean, come on. After my friend Randi visited, she told me it reminded her of Belle's little town from *Beauty and the Beast*, remarking that she felt like breaking into song as we walked down the streets, greeting shop owners and neighbors as we walked by them, reminiscent of that 1991 Disney classic's opening scene.

As I read bedtime stories to my daughter about sweet little characters going on adventures through their towns, I wondered why nobody had ever written a children's book about my own neighborhood. Besides, what a fun way to celebrate the small business owners that make our community so special. I toyed around with rhymes and phrases for a few months, and eventually, *A Magical Day in Sunnyside* was born.

I partnered with an extremely talented illustrator who happened to live only a few houses away from mine. Kate Durkin helped me bring my vision to life with her whimsical drawings portraying the story of two little girls who go on a search for magic through each of Sunnyside's shops, restaurants, and small businesses.

Somehow we were able to keep this exciting project a secret for an entire year. Then, one sunny Sunday in July, we finally had books in hand. With each of our daughters, we walked around delivering the books to every store owner, barista, and bartender whose story we had brought to life in this little book. We felt like Santa Claus on Christmas, delivering joy and tears through the town that day.

When I posted some of the photos of our special surprise deliveries to Instagram later that day, my former boss and mentor, Alex, responded with the following comment, "Amy, you have a wonderful ability to combine doing good and having fun." In that statement, she had clarified my superpower. Not writing, not marketing, not being a journalist. Those are job titles. My superpower is exactly what she articulated: doing good and having fun. The people around you often see you more clearly than you see yourself. That's why in the Curiosity Quiz and the Superpower activity, it's worth reaching out and asking. You might be delighted by what they point out.

It's easy to tap into your superpowers during times of fun and enjoyment. It's harder to draw on them during your lows. But that's actually when you need them most. Not only will your superpowers help guide you through your setback, they'll serve as a reminder of your awesomeness. They'll help you get off the damn couch. There's nothing like a confidence boost to get you moving seamlessly through the phases of a setback.

Creating a Workplace that Works for Caregivers

Blessing Adesiyan learned quickly that balancing motherhood with work would be a struggle. After all, she began her career just after she gave birth to her first child. But Adesiyan had a unique combination of superpowers that would not only help her navigate what seemed like an impossible balance—she would strive to change the workplace for all caregivers.

The seeds were planted early in her first job. After graduating college with a chemical engineering degree, Adesiyan showed up to her prestigious new job at DuPont, a Fortune 500 leader in global technology and innovation. She was just like all her new colleagues in so many ways—bright-eyed, well educated, eager to start her career at the company's West Virginia campus. But as a twenty-three-year-old Black woman, she didn't look much like her other colleagues, and when she went to pick up the security clearance materials needed for her first day on the job, she brought something her colleagues did not—her infant daughter.

Adesiyan credits that exact moment as the beginning of her decades-long quest to help large organizations support caregivers in the workplace. When she started her career, she thought, *Well, people do this all the time, so I'll figure it out.* Like so many of us, what she didn't realize was that having children and maintaining employment was possible only with layers and layers of a safety net—family nearby, disposable income to spend on childcare, and other factors not accessible to most working parents. Adesiyan gleefully sleepwalked into her setback.

A little more than half of parents say they spend more than 20 percent of their household income on childcare, according to a 2023 Care.com study.[5] Meanwhile, "89% spend 10% or more of their annual household income on child care (up from 72% in 2022.)"[6] And that's if parents can even find childcare. Over the past few years, daycare centers in the U.S. have been struggling to find, pay and retain employees. Meanwhile, across the pond, three out of four U.K. women say it does not make financial sense for them to work due to the cost of childcare.[7]

Adesiyan's managers recognized her brilliance early on. She was promoted quickly, eventually growing into a role as an operational excellence and energy solutions consultant at DuPont. But the demands of a job that required her to travel all over the world made childcare even more complicated. Despite her success, she was still a young person working through the first few years of her career. She was also an immigrant with no family in the U.S. Finding reliable and affordable childcare was a struggle. Adesiyan tried everything, from handing her baby over to her father at an airport in Morocco during a layover, to asking her neighbor to watch her daughter for an entire week. If there was a creative way to find childcare, Adesiyan had thought of it.

Someone with her level of education, talent, and drive is the exact type of employee large organizations strive to recruit and retain. But she was finding it challenging to address the demands of her job while struggling to find childcare on the side. She had worked so hard to get here, and now that she was here she was finding the balance impossible to maintain. Her setback, one she shared with caregivers across the country, was clearly Established. Despite the impact this issue was having on so many people, it felt too big, too unfixable for anyone to take on the task of figuring out what to do about it.

As Adesiyan worked through Embrace, she quickly reframed her difficulty as an opportunity. She was ready to take the reins and fix this problem others had so carelessly discarded. Why should others have to endure what she had? Why shouldn't it be possible to pursue a big career even with a young child at home?

Adesiyan entered Explore with the fierce drive and determination to figure out how to fix the broken system herself. Leave it to a single mother whose superpowers included chemical engineering training, a systems-thinking brain, and an entrepreneurial spirit to put together the building blocks that could solve the childcare crisis.

Adesiyan's biggest insight was that tools and resources already existed in the corporate world, but no one was really using them. So she tried to use what existed and build from within. Adesiyan revitalized DuPont's employee resource group (ERG) that focused on gathering parents together, voicing their concerns, and offering ideas for creative solutions from flexible hours to childcare stipends. When she eventually left DuPont for another Fortune 100 company, she tried to use what was available to reshape the system once again. But Adesiyan kept encountering the same problem—not enough support or investment to give these ERGs the chance to make any sort of impact. They were seen as volunteer activities or committees for employees to join. A setback S shape often takes the form of an obstacle course. And another one of Adesiyan's superpowers was that when she encountered obstacles, she used her systems-thinking ability to find a way over, around, or right through them.

Perhaps instead of creating or revitalizing ERGs at these large organizations, Adesiyan could create her own community of working caregivers and allow corporations to partner with them, functioning as an external ERG. It would be a way to figure out the ideal structure, build it how she envisioned it, enlist a team of her own, and then ideally make a profit selling this service into the organizations who so desperately needed it.

Adesiyan was working through Explore. It was time to see how her community could help. So she released all her frustration out onto a Post-it note.

"I was breastfeeding my four-month-old son and wrote on a Post-it note, 'What will it take for women to effectively combine work and family?'" Adesiyan recalled. "I took out another note and wrote, 'How do women return to the workforce after a baby with confidence?'"[8]

She posted a photo of her scribbled questions on Instagram before bed one night and woke up to hundreds of comments. She suggested a coffee meetup for those interested in connecting to discuss how to explore these ideas further.

To her shock and delight, when she arrived at the coffee shop in Detroit, Michigan, where she was living at the time, it was packed with working mothers all wanting to talk to her.

That's what lit up her drive to explore something bigger than just conversations over coffee. She Emerged from her setback and created that external ERG. She called it Mother Honestly and it functioned as a virtual platform with access to resources, articles, and a space for, well, honest, conversations about caregiving with a focus on finding solutions.

While Reshma Saujani is advocating for local and federal policy that supports caregivers whether they work outside the home or not, Blessing Adesiyan is trying to bring about change within the corporate world to demonstrate the value of keeping caregivers engaged and thriving within the workforce.

Adesiyan pointed out that the care crisis extends beyond birthing parents, despite moms often being the focus of caregiving and workplace initiatives. She did exactly that when she first created Mother Honestly, hence the name. But a few years later, she saw a much greater need. Adesiyan wanted to build a way for companies to expand their definition of care, from offering support for parents looking to adopt a child, those seeking gender-affirming care, those seeking travel stipends for reproductive care, and more. So she expanded her company to make sure it was inclusive of all employees who give or need care, beyond just parents.

During our interview over coffee and eggs in midtown while Adesiyan was visiting New York for her third Mother Honestly Summit, her continued commitment to addressing this issue was clear. She was determined to prevent caregivers around the country from going through as many care-related setbacks as she'd had to endure herself. Even as she found her own footing, she continued working through the Setback Cycle over and over on behalf of others.

"This country has no social safety net. Seventy-two percent of employees are living paycheck to paycheck," she said as she sipped her coffee. "In order to achieve equity, we need to acknowledge that everyone needs different things. We need to make sure we give people the opportunity to manage an unexpected care crisis. From formula shortages, tampon shortages, childcare to elder care, there's no shortage of crises."[9]

One of the solutions Adesiyan and her team came up with was something called the Care Wallet. Turns out, many large organizations have all kinds of employee assistance programs that offer benefits and stipends, but less than 6 percent of employees use them.[10]

"Workplaces offer all kinds of things like [resources] for mental health [support], gym memberships, backup childcare and more, but almost no one is using those resources," Adesiyan said. "The clunky processes frustrate employees so much that they just give up trying to use them. It's difficult to get reimbursement for costs that can be covered through stipends... or for employees to navigate the system."

Case in point: Adesiyan spoke with a dad at a Fortune 10 company that offered a $3,000 stipend for childcare. He fully planned to submit all his receipts, got sick, and missed the deadline.

My marketing agency always offered phone bill reimbursement and a monthly wellness stipend. In nearly a decade of working there, I submitted a receipt for reimbursement maybe once or twice. The process was too clunky and I never bothered. Turns out, I wasn't alone.

Adesiyan's vision now goes beyond ERGs and employee reimbursement programs. "We are building a care ecosystem. It goes beyond mothers because care is not a women's issue," she said. "All employees are impacted by care at some level. My needs as a parent are different from your needs as a single woman, or single man, or an LGBTQ+ family. That gives us the opportunity to tailor employer benefits to our unique and specific needs."[11]

Despite all she's seen and experienced firsthand, Adesiyan remains optimistic. "I do believe that the future of work is care," she said. "When employers lean into care they see more productivity, more loyalty from employees, and it truly affects the bottom line."[12]

She thinks it's possible that we will one day live in a world where more organizations begin to acknowledge that caregiving employees are worth investing in. She wants to see a future where parents and caregivers of all kinds can proudly embrace that title. That's what she's working so hard to build.

"I walked into my career with my daughter on my hips," Adesiyan said. "But that has not stopped my career from growing. I faced challenges but I saw them as an opportunity to change the workforce."[13]

Blessing Adesiyan Setback Cycle Snapshot

Phase 1: ESTABLISH	Adesiyan showed up to her first day of work as a wide-eyed college graduate with an infant on her hip. With no extended family in the country or resources for childcare, she was unsure if she'd be able to create the career she'd worked so hard to break into after all those years of schooling.
Phase 2: EMBRACE	She tried to balance working motherhood by relying on the kindness of neighbors and her parents, who would meet her at airports around the world to pick up her child as she traveled for work. She knew this wasn't sustainable. Applying a growth mindset, she was ready to take the reins and fix this problem others had so carelessly discarded.
Phase 3: EXPLORE	Adesiyan cultivated her Curiosity to address the concerns of other working moms, who, like her, kept running into impossible circumstances trying to balance childcare with work. She drew on her experiences in various workplaces and used her superpower of systems-thinking as a chemical engineer to connect the dots of what companies were willing to offer and what employees truly needed in terms of all care—not just childcare. She turned to her community and was overwhelmed by a groundswell of support. Would it be possible to fix this issue and find a viable solution that would work for everyone?

Phase 4: EMERGE	Adesiyan left the corporate world and emerged from her setback to create Mother Honestly, now called MH Work-Life. Now, she works with corporate partners to help their employees make better use of available resources, building systems that work for both companies and employers with caregiving responsibilities.

Consistency Is a Superpower

"Just starting, but starting small is such a simple piece of advice," said Roshan Shah. "I ask my clients, 'What is the smallest step you can take to start working towards a bigger goal?'"

Shah's clients absolutely hate this. They want the rocket ship, not the long ladder. Nothing gets them more frustrated than when she suggests they start small and move slowly.

"But consistency is a superpower," she said. "It is the key to getting us everything we want. And how you get to consistency is by taking small actions over and over and over again."

Consistency is a superpower because it's what makes us form new habits. Practice and repetition eventually reduce the amount of effort something takes. Once a habit is formed, it becomes more of an automatic behavior, freeing up energy in your brain.[14]

"The brain is so expensive," Chantel Prat said. "It's so energetically demanding. Sometimes you're more motivated than other times. Did you get enough sleep? Have you been making hard decisions all day long? All that physical energy impacts our motivation."

Superpowers also need fuel. They need to be identified, honored, and celebrated, especially during happy times, so you can more easily draw on them during the tougher moments. But they also have an Achilles' heel. At a workplace retreat a few years ago, my team did a superpower exercise, and the one that came up strongest for me was energy. I have a lot of it. When I told Shoshanna Hecht this, she pushed me further. "If your superpower is high energy, how do you use that?"

she asked. "Does that mean you say yes to everything, or does that mean you have to work hard to be judicious with those yeses because you're inclined to say yes too much?"

She nailed it. I'm a recovering people pleaser, a kid of the '90s who was told I could—and should—be able to "do it all." I often take on more than my bandwidth allows. That means I absolutely say yes to too many things. My energy, the very thing that our team bonding game revealed to be one of my superpowers, gets quickly depleted.

While celebrating your superpowers is important, it's also critical to understand the structures and systems that can make our super-powers work against us.

"Your superpower is what is important to you and what you're motivated to do," Prat said, "But adjudicating between that and what society says is valuable is tricky. Power and money are society's metric of success, but striving for those things just makes you stressed and sick. Stress kills creativity. A brain under pressure gives you a narrow sense of possibility."

And we need to make sure that sense of possibility remains expansive. As we work our way out of Explore and into Emerge, we'll need to focus our superhero vision on one of the most critical pieces needed to reach the end of the Setback Cycle—our community.

CHAPTER 7

A Call for Community

"Social connection is a form of nourishment, like food," Emily and Amelia Nagoski point out in *Burnout*.[1] "Our specific nutritional needs change over the course of our life span, but the fundamental need for food does not; similarly, our need for connection changes across our life spans, but our fundamental need for connection does not."

If social connection is nourishment, isolation and loneliness are hunger and thirst.

The past decade has seen a shift in social interactions as more of our connecting happens in digital worlds, from text messages to DMs to passively scrolling. Psychologists and the United States surgeon general sounded the alarms in 2022 that society is in the midst of a loneliness epidemic that has been negatively impacting our mental and physical health and even our life expectancy.[2]

Over the years of interviewing founders, I've heard stories that flow along the lines of, "I tried this thing, it totally failed, everything was terrible, I didn't know what to do."

But inevitably, that golden nugget moment is almost always community-oriented. They land on the conclusion that if they are struggling with something, there's a decent chance other people are too. That realization is often the birthplace of great ideas. And those great ideas turn into solutions that benefit entire communities.

As we prepare to truly emerge from the Setback Cycle, community is critical. Putting a new idea out into the world is scary. Asking for help is hard. Draw on your friends and family to serve as your personal advisory board. Get a hype squad—people to boost your confidence so you can do the scary thing. Also, enlist a challenge network—people who respectfully point out flaws in service of making your idea better and seeing you truly succeed.

My hype squad and challenge network allowed me to write this book.

You think writing is a solitary endeavor? There's no way you'd be reading this (or listening to it) right now if I hadn't called my friend Ruthie one gray March morning and heard her say, "Yes, this should be a book." It was my green light to start. I turned to people who were willing to read, edit, and share honest thoughts in service of making these words even better. I don't think creativity can exist without community.

See Your Community as a Constellation

Susan McPherson is known as a serial connector who starts every interaction with, "How can I help you?" She's also the author of *The Lost Art of Connecting,* where she talks about the concept of seeing communities as constellations. "Each person is a piece of a larger vision: for you, for them, and for global issues we face as a society," she told me over the phone.

That constellation imagery of 250 billion stars in the galaxy helps us envision ourselves as part of a larger picture. "But you never know just how you are connected to another person until you put in the work to see the patterns," she notes in her book.[3]

In antiquity, our ancestors looked up at the sky to make sense of things. That's essentially what led them to create the constellations. If you look at a map of the galaxies and stars, you'll notice that many of the constellations overlap. Our communities are more intertwined than we realize.

"The constellation concept is all about this notion that when we make introductions, we're leading to impact," McPherson said. She advises people going through challenges to map out who they want to meet and see how they might be indirectly connected to those people.

When we connect with people, it helps us make sense of the world. We can find new perspectives, get new ideas, or just have someone validate that we haven't completely lost our minds (or help us out if we have.) There's no better way to derive meaning from chaos than by talking to the people in your constellation.

I asked McPherson about the role she thought our communities could play as we work through the Setback Cycle. She paused for a moment, before saying, "I can't imagine any other way to get through setbacks."

Consider weddings and funerals. When we celebrate the best or endure the hardest things in life, we immediately turn to our communities, and they turn to us to offer support.

But not all of us are inclined to reach out when we perhaps should. Some of us are guarded and don't want to share a new idea or venture until it's absolutely perfect, some of us are afraid of failure, and some of us simply don't want to ask for help.

"I don't care if you're a Fortune 500 CEO or a taxi driver," she said. "We all have things to offer each other. I realize someone who is feeling insecure or coming out of a setback might feel hesitant to ask for help, but there's never any hurt in trying."

A no is always going to be a no if you never bother to ask.

"For the people who are worried about being an imposition, it's important to remember that what you're doing is offering somebody a tremendous opportunity to give a gift," McPherson said. "People love being made to feel useful. When others ask for help, and someone can actually provide that help, it's a wonderful feeling."

McPherson is one of the most well connected, and busiest, entrepreneurs on the planet, and yet she is delighted when people ask her to make a connection for them. "When people come to me and say they want to meet someone, I immediately feel valued," she said, "because I'm part of the food chain."

"Plus, when you make an introduction between two people, you never know the magic that's going to happen," she said.

I couldn't agree more. My former boss and mentor Adrianna always tells me that New York City is "six degrees of Amy Sho." She's been telling me this since I was a not-at-all-well-connected twenty-six-year-old starting out in my career. I always laughed because while sure, I would run into a friend here and there, I thought she was simply exaggerating. Looking back, I realize perhaps she saw my constellation as it was just beginning to form.

"When you build relationships that are not static, temporary or limited to a particular project or venture, you never know what can emerge," McPherson says.

Making "Good Trouble"

Nicole Stipp and Kaitlyn Soligan had been best friends since meeting in Washington, D.C. as they were just starting their careers. They bonded, as many twenty-somethings in D.C. did, over their love for whiskey and their shared vision of what an idealistic world could look like.

Those budding careers took them both to New York City, where they bunked up in a Harlem apartment. Over a decade later, Soligan made another big move—her romantic partner had grown up in Louisville, Kentucky, and told Soligan how much better the cost of living was in his hometown. Eventually, he convinced her to move back there with him.

Though Soligan was excited for her new life, she couldn't help but feel a bit out of place. She often found herself wishing she had a community of her own in her new city.

Soligan Established a small S curve setback as she struggled at first to find community in Louisville. Stipp was also a midwesterner, having grown up in Indiana. To help Soligan Embrace her new reality and settle into her new location, Stipp visited frequently. It was during those visits when Soligan found herself seeking out a part of Louisville culture she often felt excluded from. On those visits, the duo would sign up for tours around the area's distilleries, learning about Louisville's rich whiskey and bourbon history. They were among the only women in these travel groups, as the Kentucky whiskey scene was, and still is, predominantly male. On those early trips, Stipp and Soligan would dream up ways to create these types of experiences for women, people of color, and other folks who had perhaps felt out of place at Kentucky's premier drinking establishments.

"We started to wonder: Is this something we could create ourselves?" recalled Stipp. They became more curious as they entered Explore.

That Curiosity turned into a capital C as Stipp made the decision, after years of long distance-scheming, to give up her New York apartment and return to her midwestern roots. She had to first process a bit of an identity shift that came with leaving the city she took so much pride in calling home, but at the same time, she was ready for a change. She packed her bags for Louisville to go into business with her friend.

Soligan was elated. "I thought, 'Wow, I might actually get to be happy here in Louisville,'" she said.

For the first few months, Stipp slept on Soligan's floor, spending lots of time snuggling with Soligan's dog. "It was a very nice floor," Stipp laughed.

Together, they spent their days following their Curiosity and working through Explore as they researched the local bourbon and whiskey industry. They talked to everyone they could within the local community, asking tons of questions. They were determined to learn as much as they could about the industry, the local market, and what they could build to fill the gap of what they felt was missing.

"Hospitality is, at its core, making people feel included and welcome," said Stipp. As two Louisville newcomers, that's exactly what they set out to do.

Their travel company, Matson & Gilman, named after two trail-blazing whiskey women, launched in 2016. Esther Matson was caught bootlegging whiskey in the 1700s, so the twenty-two-year-old was "sentenced to church every Sunday for two years."[4] Lavinia Gilman was an eighty-year-old Montana woman who, during prohibition, was caught and arrested for running a three-hundred-gallon still.[5]

About a year and a half in, Stipp and Soligan started to notice a shift in requests from travelers. "They were less interested in seeing multiple distilleries in one day," Stipp shared, "and much more interested in tasting and learning about their own palate."

To accommodate these requests, Stipp started hosting whiskey tastings out of the trunk of her car. As lovely as her car was, the duo decided to upgrade the experience for travelers and invest in a permanent tasting room.

When the journey to find a space for their new venture yielded frustrating results, they almost gave up.

But one day, while Soligan was back home for Thanksgiving, Stipp finally found the perfect spot. Soligan was skeptical, but humored Stipp and agreed to FaceTime. When she saw the space, even through that small iPhone screen, Soligan realized that they had just been looking for the wrong thing. Stipp wasn't showing her a tasting room. It was a bar in downtown Louisville, in a neighborhood that was starting to see a huge rebirth. They could open the first women-owned whiskey bar in the area. "The bar just told us what it needed to grow up to be," Soligan remembered. They had entered the Emerge phase of the Setback Cycle. Trouble Bar opened in August 2019.

Stipp and Soligan set out to make Trouble Bar a pub that specialized in whiskey, but also honored the tradition of pubs being public houses for the community. They sought to create an inclusive and welcoming place for women and other marginalized groups in Louisville who, like them, had not felt so welcome at other whiskey establishments.

"Trouble Bar is a beacon of our values for a more just, more equitable, and more diverse community," said Stipp.

"We are attuned to what it's like to move through a world that can be pretty unequal," Stipp said. "We have family members with disabilities, so we know how it feels to try and scout out a restaurant or bar to make sure they could accommodate limited mobility. We have trans friends who had told us how weird it was to try and decide which bathroom they could safely use in places that require gendered bathrooms."

The Wall of Trouble was the first thing I noticed when I first interviewed Stipp and Soligan over Zoom. When you walk into the sunlight-filled bar with its exposed brick walls and inviting upholstered green chairs, it is this photography installation that first catches your eye.

"We wanted to pay tribute to folks in history who have shaken the world with their 'good trouble,'" said Stipp. Photos of troublemakers like John Lewis, Harvey Milk, and Leslie Feinberg lined the wall.

They also offer their space to local community activists and nonprofits, waiving the rental fee or bar minimum to host gatherings. "We both worked in nonprofits and remember how hard it was to just find a space where you could host twenty folks and either raise money or just build community," Stipp remembered. "We set out to hire a super diverse team and our beverage director is one of the few Black women to hold that title in Louisville. We don't simply do those things to check boxes, we do them because we believe it makes our space better, more inclusive and more welcoming."

THE SETBACK CYCLE

Kaitlyn Soligan Setback Cycle Snapshot (1 of 2)

Phase 1: ESTABLISH	Kaitlyn Soligan left her friends behind and struggled to find community as she built her new life in Louisville.
Phase 2: EMBRACE	Soligan froze and got caught up in rumination, convinced she could never be happy in Louisville. Her best friend, Nicole Stipp, came to visit frequently. Those visits are what thawed Soligan out. They would move around the city, get fresh air, and familiarize themselves with the area. They toured the city's bourbon and whiskey scenes as part of this thaw. And they couldn't help but notice the experience felt like it was missing something.
Phase 3: EXPLORE	These experiences piqued their Curiosity as they started to ask around to see if others felt the way they had on their own whiskey and bourbon tours around Louisville. Soligan and Stipp knew what their superpowers were—building things from scratch, noticing when experiences weren't inclusive or representative of all groups—and cultivating community.
Phase 4: EMERGE	With a nod to their early, idealistic days in D.C., the duo considered how they could create something to benefit the community in Louisville and address these very homogenous travel and tourism experiences. Stipp decided to make her own big move to Louisville, where the two created Matson & Gilman, a whiskey tourism company catered toward marginalized groups, then expanded to create Trouble Bar—a space for connection and comfort that addressed what Soligan was originally seeking—inclusion, belonging, and community.

The two had recognized the power of forging a community, and were on a mission to broaden their constellation in a new city. Less than a year after Trouble Bar's grand opening, they would need to rely on that community to get through their toughest setback yet.

Connect With Your Constellation

Some people really struggle to explore the depths of their constellation. They feel uncomfortable striking up a conversation with a stranger or even reaching out to someone they haven't spoken to in a while. Daniel Pink, author of *The Power of Regret,* said in an interview on Maya Shankar's podcast *A Slight Change of Plans,* that loss of connection is a top-four regret of people at the end of their lives.

"When people tell you what they regret the most, they're telling you what they value the most," said Pink. "Connection regrets are regrets about relationships...certain relationships just drift apart. Then one person wants to reach out, but they think, 'It's been ten years, it's going to be so awkward.' So we wait another few years, and then it's even more awkward to reach out. That ends up being a colossal mistake on both fronts, because when we do reach out it's always way less awkward than we think and the other side almost always cares."[6]

The power of connection is so strong, it can also add years to your life. "Confidants, friends, acquaintances, co-workers, relatives, spouses, and companions all provide a life-enhancing social net—and may increase longevity," according to Harvard Health Publishing. "It's not clear why, but the buffering theory holds that people who enjoy close relationships with family and friends receive emotional support that indirectly helps to sustain them at times of chronic stress and crisis."[7]

The British government went as far as appointing a Minister for Loneliness to address concerns around feelings of disconnection. As part of this effort, they set up simple ways for people to easily interact.[8] One town set up "Happy to Chat" benches, with signs reading "Sit here if you don't mind chatting with someone new," and "See someone here? Join them to chat!"[9] This experiment was so well received that other countries like Canada and Poland ended up creating similar programs.

We value connections more than we may realize. Even the most introverted among us. So how do we start exploring those connections in a more meaningful way, especially when doing so means expanding beyond our usual level of comfort?

You don't have to focus on building deep, intimate relationships right off the bat. Consider the light-touch interactions you can have with casual acquaintances. The other parent who laughs with the kids at school drop-off, the barista you see every morning who knows your order, a neighbor who walks their dog at the same time you do. These "weak ties" can actually be a critical antidote to feeling disconnected. Defined as "infrequent, arms-length relationships," according to research from MIT, Stanford, Harvard, and LinkedIn, "weak ties" can even be more beneficial for employment opportunities, promotions, and wages than strong ties.[10]

They can also offer low-stakes practice in striking up conversations and sharpening that Curiosity muscle (great for exploring both your big C and little c curiosities.) Plus, there's always a chance those weak ties can develop into stronger ones.

McPherson advises that if people want to reach out and make a connection with someone specific, they should start small, with an email, a LinkedIn message, or a direct message and introduce themselves by asking how they can help or support the work the other person is doing. Just say hello. Start with a mutual interest, offer to support them however you can, don't ask for anything, and allow the relationship to grow from there.

Connect with Your Constellation

How do you start making those deeper connections? Instead of asking, "What do you do?" when you first meet a person, McPherson suggests starting with one of the following. It also helps to have these prompts handy if you find yourself in an awkward pause in conversation:

- How are you spending your time these days?
- If you could be anywhere in the world next week, where would it be and why?
- What was your favorite food as a child? (You get so much more than naming a dish out of this question!)
- What was the last best podcast you listened to?
- If you were going to solve one world problem, and money wasn't an issue, what would it be?

"These types of things give you a vision into who the other person truly is, what their passions are and what lights them up," McPherson said, "But they're not so personal that you're going to make somebody feel uncomfortable if you ask them."

This may seem obvious but it's worth stating that all relationships, even the weak ties, need to be two-sided. Another way to strengthen the relationships between you and those in your community is to sharpen your listening skills. Try to be a good listener as often as you can. If you realize you've been taking too much air time in a conversation or you see a lot of text messages coming from you, pause and let others respond. Ask them questions. Then truly listen to what they have to say. Listening is one of the most important and, in my opinion, under taught skills when it comes to interpersonal relationships.

McPherson suggests making a list of the people you feel most comfortable reaching out to and starting there. Send one email a day, one text a day, make one phone call a day. I know, "you're not a phone person." But this takes thirty seconds and the benefits are immeasurable.

When I think of how much I've mapped my constellation over the years, exploring its nooks, crannies and galaxies, I can trace a lot of those connections back to my early years of volunteering with an organization called She's the First, which serves to ensure girls across the world have access to education, breaking generational cycles of poverty. I'm still close with the founder, Tammy Tibbetts, and in fact, the publishing of this book was able to benefit that organization and their mission. Your reading this is helping send a girl to school, and that's amazing because think of what girls can do when they are educated, respected, and heard.

If you're looking to build connections, or expand your constellation, but don't know where to start, I highly recommend volunteering, joining a sports league or hosting a game night. Working together toward a shared goal forms incredibly strong bonds and fosters a sense of community.

"Nothing worth doing is easy, even building a constellation," McPherson (who, interestingly enough, is one of the wonderful people who I met during those early days at She's the First) said. "It always takes that first step—finding that first link to another star—but the payoff, when it works, is huge."

Turning Lemons into Lemonade

By early 2020, only a few months after opening Trouble Bar, business was skyrocketing. Stipp and Soligan had just thrown a memorable New Year's Eve party, and were having what Stipp described as "one of the most epic first quarters."

"Sales were really exceeding anything we had predicted and we felt like we were heading into a truly outstanding spring and summer," she recalled. After all those years of starts and stops, all the hard work, the challenges and the triumphs, they had forged an enormous, supportive community.

As they scrolled through news stories that March, they knew Trouble Bar could certainly be in trouble. It wasn't much of a shock when on March 16, 2020, Kentucky's governor, Andy Beshear, announced that he was restricting the sale of liquor and not allowing anyone to drink on the premises of restaurants and bars. The duo's next setback had been Established. They would have to work through the cycle once again.

One afternoon in those early, hazy days of the pandemic with a ban on liquor sales, Soligan remembered that they had just stocked up on juices and mixers. In the midst of Embrace, Stipp and Soligan adjusted their expectations of what they needed to keep the bar afloat, and tried to figure out how they could still connect with their community without the ability to gather in a physical space.

Together, they came up with a brilliant idea. Stipp and Soligan made lemons into lemonade, in the most literal sense. They opened up a lemonade stand just outside of the bar, and were blown away by how many people showed up for them, offering donations, making postcards to help spread the word, and, of course, buying lemonade. Their loyal community was determined to do all they could to support the business owners who had created the space where they could all feel welcome. Tough times force you to adopt a growth mindset and draw on your creativity in ways you may never have been able to imagine.

"I still can't believe we created an actual lemonade stand," Soligan laughed. "A local print shop made us prints that said, 'When life hands you lemons, make trouble.' The first two or three lemonade stands were so successful that I realized, we might just be able to pay one month of bills from this."

Stipp and Soligan were clear on their mission. From their early days of Matson & Gilman to the most bountiful days of Trouble Bar's success, their superpower had always been cultivating community. It's what got them through the Explore phase during the pandemic. And it was that exact community that lifted them up when they needed it the most. When Trouble Bar opened back up six months later, they had finally Emerged once again, and the energy in the space was palpable. I spoke to Stipp and Soligan that June over Zoom, just as they were preparing for a big Pride celebration, one of the only bars in town to do so.

Their Zoom backdrop was a rainbow balloon arch. "It's like Pride threw up in here," Stipp joked as she sat in the exact space they had always envisioned and worked so hard to maintain.

The Complications of Cultivating Community

That Pride celebration would be a lovely bow to tie the end of their story with, and I wish I could tell you that evening's celebration was their happy ending. But as with any business, the road is full of bumps. Ironically, one of the bumps they faced later on was finding a driver to help them navigate those bumpy local roads.

Shortly after Trouble Bar reopened and people started socializing in person again, Louisville saw a huge boom in tourism. Stipp and Soligan decided this might be the perfect moment to expand their travel business, Matson & Gilman, which they were still running. Perhaps instead of doing the packaged tours they had been running for years, they could dip a whiskey-soaked toe into the bespoke travel industry. They opened M&G Excursions a few months later, creating customized experiences specifically for the same marginalized communities who were still being excluded from bourbon tourism marketing.

Stipp and Soligan were considerate of what some of these overlooked audiences might be craving when researching travel, specifically for those travelers who may have been a bit extra worried about the safety of their visits, and whether or not tour guides would treat them with respect and camaraderie.

However, the influx of tourism to the area meant an influx of demand for drivers.

"And those drivers aren't always sensitive to the needs of the travelers we attract," said Stipp.

I asked her what she meant by that. "Some drivers aren't comfortable with a woman talking about bourbon and they jump in to explain things to the guide we hired," she said. "We are at the mercy of these companies because they own most of the sprinter vans in town. But we keep finding ourselves in this continuously weird dynamic."

Stipp and Soligan considered buying their own large sprinter van to take their tour groups around, but as they stared down an economic recession and thought about the credit card debt they had gone into to keep Trouble Bar afloat once the PPP relief ran out, it seemed out of reach.

Running a hospitality business is not for the faint of heart. Cash flow issues continue to force the duo to make tough decisions every day. But they're committed to their mission, and to their community. So they keep showing up and getting creative in order to keep their business going. Stipp and Soligan are deeply proud of what they built, and are determined to enable Trouble Bar to serve as a gathering space for those in their community, even if it's not something that can support them financially.

Stipp and Soligan sometimes turn to freelance marketing as a way to help bring in income and pay their bills when the bar and the travel company face dips in revenue. Coincidentally, Susan McPherson, the serial connector, has hired Stipp for a few consulting jobs, something I was not aware of when I paired them in this chapter. Talk about the power of community. McPherson truly abides by her principles of connection and offers to help those in her constellation. The last time I interviewed Stipp, she was considering reaching back out to McPherson to see if she might be open to working together again.

Stipp and Soligan are constantly finding new ways to deliver on their promise to Louisville tourists and loyal Trouble Bar customers while they look ahead to what their next move might be. No matter what the future holds, Stipp and Soligan will always center their ventures around supporting their community.

A successful business relies on its constellation.

A Sliver of Societal Progress

The overturning of *Roe v. Wade* had a deep impact in Kentucky, one of a dozen states whose trigger laws went into effect immediately following the ruling, which severely restricted women's access to reproductive healthcare across the state.

It wasn't just Kentucky. Less than one year after the ruling, twenty-four states had rolled back access to women's health.

But out of that devastating moment also came a burst of energy around protecting those most impacted by the new ruling. A few months later, the Kentucky state legislature was about to vote on a constitutional amendment that would have created a full abortion ban in the state. Antichoice groups campaigned for months to try to get the amendment to pass.[11]

Stipp has always been vocal about a woman's right to make decisions about her own reproductive care, trying to destigmatize the conversation by candidly sharing the story of her own abortion. Once again she used her superpower of gathering people together over a shared mission. She got the word out to some of the more progressive voters in the area and rallied people to speak out against the passing of this amendment. When it came time for the vote, it did not pass. Stipp is deeply proud of the work her community did to organize voters in a very conservative, deeply religious state.

"That amendment didn't pass because more people showed up to vote than ever before," she said. "And this was not a national election cycle."

It was yet another example of a community springing into action to fuel progress.

Your community is always ready to celebrate your wins and offer you access to the resources you need—a friendly face, a shoulder to cry on, someone to laugh with, someone to protest with. And if you're lucky, your constellation includes a bar owner or two.

Nicole Stipp and Kaitlyn Soligan Setback Cycle Snapshot (2 of 2)

Phase 1: ESTABLISH	Trouble Bar was created as a gathering place in the tradition of public houses to form a community and create a safe space for those who felt unwelcome in other whiskey establishments. But when Soligan and Stipp had to close their bar at the beginning of the pandemic, that safe space was threatened. How could they stay afloat while gathering and the sale of liquor were banned in Louisville for the foreseeable future?
Phase 2: EMBRACE	Stipp and Soligan adjusted their expectations of what they needed to keep the bar afloat, and applied a growth mindset to figure out how they could show up for their community without a physical space.
Phase 3: EXPLORE	They tapped into their superpowers of creativity, coming up with the idea to turn lemons into lemonade. Stipp and Soligan turned their recently purchased juices and mixes into a lemonade stand. They showed up for their community by creating a space for them, and when gathering in that space wasn't allowed, it was their community who showed up for them.
Phase 4: EMERGE	When the world opened back up, Trouble Bar remained a safe place to gather once again. Stipp and Soligan emerged from that period with an even more loyal constellation as they had forged new bonds working through that tough period together. They continue to support their community through the inevitable setbacks that arise, knowing they'll get through whatever comes next—together.

The Explore phase can be pretty fun. Self-awareness, the willingness to excavate your deep-rooted Curiosity, ask hard questions of yourself and others, draw on your superpowers, connect with your constellation and rally those around you for support will be key to moving forward as you complete the cycle and Emerge like a phoenix from your setback.

PHASE 4
EMERGE

CHAPTER 8

There's No Place Like Home

We've made it to *Emerge*. We have rearranged our caterpillar parts, peeked out of our chrysalis, and are ready to spread our beautiful new wings. Completing the Setback Cycle in the Emerge phase is exhilarating after reconnecting more deeply with your Curiosity, your superpowers, and your community in *Explore*. You have the tools, you've tuned into your creativity and strengths, and now it's time to decide what to build. This is where many reach that critical and coveted turning point.

"I've processed my setback and have an understanding of my options. But now what?" Shoshanna Hecht said. "This is where the rubber hits the road and taking action is the hardest. This is where people say, 'You know what, maybe I'll go back to bed. Maybe tomorrow.'"

Going from planning to doing can be scary but liberating. Emerge is when we have to fly away and leave the comfort of our chrysalis, or for some of us, our couch, and put that plan into action. The couch can be so damn cozy, though.

Getting Off the Couch

So how do we get over that little bit of leftover fear of moving forward when we get to Emerge?

"You know the drill," Dr. Casarella said. "Once you deal with the logical steps of determining what you need to do, you have to deal with the feelings."

Ugh. This again? Didn't we do enough "feeling" during Embrace?

Am I uncomfortable actually doing this thing? Will it take me away from other things? What's the risk? Will I still get to see my children? Will I still feel like myself? How will this shift the roles I play in all of my relationships?

There's a lot of talk about slowing down to speed up and taking rest when you need it. Maybe it's time for a breather now that you've done the work and need a moment before you lurch forward. That's okay. Take the break. Take a nap. Digest the growth.

"Sometimes there's no psychological explanation for it," said Dr. Casarella. In more clinical terms, she added, "Sometimes, your body is just fucking tired."

"Doing the thing can be hard," Roshan Shah said. "It's much easier to realize you're facing those barriers. It's much harder to give yourself the grace to step around them. Moving into action is harder, because we struggle so much with giving ourselves grace."

Ah, yes: giving ourselves grace as we climb out of the gray. We have landed in Oz, and the door to the world of color is right in front of us. All we have to do is open the door.

From Hudson Yards to an Extended Homecoming

In late 2019, chef Palak Patel was tenaciously working to achieve her dream of opening her own restaurant in New York City. The Atlanta native had secured a space in the brand new, beautiful Hudson Yards complex on the far west side of Manhattan. After living in New York for a decade and winning reality show fame from her stints on *Food Network Star*, *Chopped*, and *Beat Bobby Flay*, she had several investors and half a million dollars lined up to support the grand opening of her long-awaited space. She was elated that after years of hard work, she was going to do the very thing food lovers and chefs around the world dream of doing.

Only a few short months later, as she was in the process of picking out fixtures and appliances in early 2020, she got a phone call. Restaurants were being told to shut down. Her opening would be delayed until everyone figured out what was happening.

As the fate of the restaurant industry grew uncertain amid pandemic shutdowns, Patel packed a single backpack and hopped on a plane to Atlanta to stay with her parents. She thought she would be back to New York in a month or so.

As the weeks went by and New York became the epicenter, Patel started to realize her life was changing, perhaps permanently. The first investors called, terrified of what the future held. One by one, they regrettably pulled out of their commitments to her as the restaurant industry pause seemed to be going on indefinitely. After a decade of working toward her dream, as that coveted finish line was just within her grasp, it all completely fell apart.

Like so many adults in the pandemic, Patel thought her visit to Atlanta was temporary. Spending those early, uncertain months in her childhood bedroom, the forty-something-year-old chef embraced the pause. She took the forced reset for what it was—a moment to reflect and revise. She meditated and did yoga every single day as she mourned her old life and worried about her future and the future of the restaurant industry at large. Patel had always felt a sense of pride when people asked her where she lived. "Leaving New York City, no longer having the Hudson Yards restaurant, to me, felt like failing," she said. "But I knew that was just my ego."

"Every New Yorker thinks they're going to die when that zip code goes away," she added wryly, "But I had to step into the new change in the world and in me."

After months of introspection and healing, Patel was able to see that the only person putting New York on a pedestal and giving it so much value was herself. Over the following year, she came to accept what she calls "the shattering of my life," and acknowledged that it happened in the best possible way.

"No one really talks about the sticky stuff," she said. "When you hear someone's success story, you always hear about the shiny, glossy thing they created. But it doesn't work like that."

Welcome to the Setback Cycle, chef.

Patel's move from New York to Atlanta grounded her more than she initially realized it would. In New York, she was always chasing something. Here, at home, she could just be.

Opening that door to the world of color might be beautiful and exciting, but as it turns out there's really no place like home.

"You can't compare New York and Atlanta, but I realize now that it is incredibly dangerous to loop in your identity to a place or lifestyle," she said. "That's a very slippery slope. I had fallen so deeply into that, that I didn't realize it, until one day, back in my childhood bedroom in Atlanta, I finally woke up."

Patel, like so many others, knew she still had to move forward, but was frozen in place. She wasn't sure when she would feel fully prepared to take that first small step into the unknown. What would she do next? What would society do next?

She put it best when she said, "You have to burn this shit down to build it back up again."

Intuitive Decision-Making

Planning and plotting is a great way to gain clarity around a difficult situation, but also, trust your instincts. You have what the Nagoski sisters call an internal "monitor." Your monitor "knows what your goal is, how much effort you're investing in that goal, and how much progress you're making."[1]

When our monitor notices that a project, a relationship, or a situation is taking a lot of our energy, time, and investment and we are making very little progress toward a goal, we might end up switching the goal from the attainable category to unattainable. This is what makes us want to quit.

"It pushes you off an emotional cliff into a pit of despair," they say. "Lost in helplessness, your brain abandons hope."

Palak Patel sat in this moment for a time before she could move forward. But Patel always trusted her instincts. She was waiting until the right plan revealed itself to her.

Luckily, there's also something called "positive reappraisal," which is our conscious ability to switch our monitor back to a place where we decide that the effort, even though it may be fraught with discomfort, frustration, and difficulty, is still worth it.

"Even the repeated failure has value," the sisters say, "Not just because they are steps toward a worthwhile goal, but because you reframe difficulties as opportunities for growth and learning."[2]

Not to be confused with toxic positivity (this is not the time to put on a happy face and pretend everything is fine—that helps no one), positive reappraisal is a way to motivate your mind to walk back from that cliff.

Intention versus Impact

I like to think we all have the best intentions. But intention doesn't always lead to impact. Even when we know what we should be doing, our actions don't automatically follow suit. How many doctors do you know who smoke? "Do as I say, not as I do" is a saying for that exact reason. A setback, unpleasant as it may be, can prompt us to finally act. The motivation to avoid another negative experience can be just what we need to get off the couch. Sometimes we have to let that wall crash down to see that the studs were never all that stable.

"Knowing better doesn't always lead to doing better," Chantel Prat said. "You need to use your explicit knowledge and memories to make decisions about what you think will be successful. Prior experiences tell you what's going to work and what's not."

But you're the one who has to take that information and put it into action. The best way to accommodate potential mistakes or missteps? Make a plan. And then make several backup plans.

The ABC's of Scenario Planning

When Plan A doesn't work out, it's nice to have clearly outlined plans B and C. When most people come up with an idea, they don't really go further than plan A. They put all their eggs in one basket. Or for many entrepreneurs, all their money into one business. That's why Roshan Shah recommends the ABC approach to goal setting. It provides three versions of a goal to help improve chances of success.

She explains the ABC approach like this:

Scenario Planning: The ABC Approach

- Plan A is the *Ideal Plan*—the ideal outcome you want to experience.
- Plan B is the *Backup Plan*—when you can't achieve Plan A, how can you refocus to achieve something that is more attainable and still valuable?
- Plan C is the *Safety Net* (or backup to the backup)—if neither the A nor B plan is achieved, this changes the focus again so you can still achieve something meaningful.

Shah counsels clients to write out each of their goals using this approach so they can plan for different scenarios right from the beginning. It also helps them think through multiple outcomes and yes, set realistic expectations. "This helps people from getting stuck, or falling into a shame cycle by normalizing that sometimes you might need to pivot," she said. "And that's okay! It doesn't mean all is lost or you have failed. It teaches people to be more adaptable and agile and learn the practice of, 'So that happened, what's next?' as opposed to throwing the whole goal out the window."

In other words, it won't defeat you. You can pivot to Plan B. Just make sure you know what Plan B is before you need to execute that option.

The sweet spot of goal setting is aiming high, striving for a challenge yet keeping it attainable. Most importantly, ensure that as you work toward your goal, the effort feels worth the outcome. Even if that goal changes over time.

Building from the Rubble

Patel slowly entered the Explore phase of the Setback Cycle. She may not have thoroughly scenario planned as Roshan Shah would have liked, but she had moved into Plan B. She put down roots in Atlanta, and bought a house. She had decided to stay. Every time I interviewed Patel, she spoke to me from her car as she was running errands. "Welcome to my co-working office," she joked when I pointed this out. "In Atlanta, you have to get into your car to get to your garbage can." There is no truer sign that a city lifestyle has been shed for a suburban one than someone doing business from their car.

Patel always knew what her superpower was—sharing her passion for flavor, cooking, and joyfully gathering people together over a collective love of food. She was open to whatever possibilities lie ahead. One day, her Curiosity led her and a friend to a hip new food hall that had just opened in the Underwood Hills neighborhood. While there, she came across an empty food stall. That stall opened the door to Patel's Emerge phase.

Patel scenario planned. It wasn't a sit-down restaurant as she'd always dreamed of (Plan A), but that no longer felt like the place her journey would lead. She looked at the empty food stall. Perhaps something like this could still allow her to fulfill that dream, to share her love of food with others, but in a way that was more aligned with her new life, her new values, and what felt right for her in this moment.

One year after her official move to Atlanta, Chattahoochee Food Works opened its first Indian street food stall, Dash and Chutney. There, Patel served casual food from all regions of India to the enthusiastic patrons who visited the space daily. It may not have been upscale or in a fancy zip code, but to her, Plan B was perfection.

"Building from the rubble of your old life is not easy," she said. "But I learned that things happen for you—not to you. So this setback, in a way, was the best thing that has happened to me for personal and professional growth."

By 2023, Patel was looking to move Dash and Chutney into a larger space. She still loves her life in Atlanta, though she visits New York often. "I accomplished more here in three years than I did during my ten years in New York," she said. "I wrote a cookbook, bought a house and opened a restaurant. I cultivated a better relationship with my family and a better relationship with myself."

Her metamorphosis was complete.

Palak Patel Setback Cycle Snapshot

Phase 1: ESTABLISH	After spending a decade building her visibility as a chef, courting investors, and years of careful planning, Patel's restaurant dreams were crushed in an instant. Everything she had been working toward was gone.
Phase 2: EMBRACE	She flew to her parents' house in Atlanta, meditated, reflected, and paused as she mourned the loss of her big dream. She struggled with her new life in Atlanta as she began to shed her identity as a New Yorker. She resisted embracing the new situation until one day, in her childhood bedroom, she finally "woke up."
Phase 3: EXPLORE	Patel began to dream again. She knew what her super-power was—connecting her community over a love of food. As she was trying to figure out how to parlay that into her next move, she remained adaptable even if "what's next" looked completely different from her original plan. She explored her Curiosity all the way to a new food hall, and in it, an empty food stall that beckoned her.
Phase 4: EMERGE	Patel trusted her intuition and decided to take the leap. She began to lay the foundation of her new life, brick by brick. She opened a food stall in her hometown, bought a house, and put down roots in Atlanta once again. The food stall concept was a new take on plant-based Indian-inspired street food, more casual than her original sit-down restaurant, but it felt exactly right for her. She's also about to publish her debut cookbook that celebrates her favorite recipes. She stayed true to her North Star, and through her comeback, Patel was able to find new, creative ways to share her love of food with the world.

CHAPTER 9

Your Decision-Making Framework

How do you know what to do when faced with a monumental decision? Where and how do we start laying those bricks? The Emerge phase commences with the defining question: what now?

If you're a Libra like me, you exist in a sea of indecision. My friend once gifted me a Magic 8 Ball as a joke, but reader, that thing has helped me make more decisions than I care to admit.

In order to prevent this process from becoming too overwhelming, it's best to start small.

"If you have an idea of where you want to go, you can start to roadmap it," Shoshanna Hecht says. She suggests starting with the least important to most important as you plan out the process, using a small-step decision-making framework.

"Begin with an end in mind," she said. "You don't have to set it in stone. It can evolve, because we are human. But pick a point. I like five years. It's not too soon, but it's not too far. Do you want to still be slogging away at your job? Where will your kids be? Where will your partner be? Do you want a bigger house, do you want a car? Mind map whatever works for you."

Hecht suggests using the framework of "Have, Do, Be." Identifying what you want to have, what you want to do and who you want to be at that future moment in time will allow you to get clear on what's important. That can serve as the driving force behind how you evaluate decisions, big and small. And remember, you are always allowed to adjust. Do not etch this framework in stone. (If you have that skill, though, I'm impressed; let's chat.) Let it evolve as you do. But put something in place based on what you hope to work toward.

"When you are connected to those drivers, choices are easy," Hecht said. "It also makes it a lot easier to set boundaries if you are really connected to why on earth you're doing anything."

Small-Step Decision-Making Framework

Have + Do + Be

1. In five years, what do you want to *have*?
2. What do you want to be *doing*? How do you want to be spending most of your time?
3. In five years, who will you *be*?

Now let's get granular. Write out a big goal. Then break it down into smaller, more manageable steps. If this goal is something like launching your own business, what are the twenty steps you need to take to get there? Start to consider the details.

- What resources will you need to get started on day one?
- If you need to leave a job in order to start that business, list out the things you need to confidently walk out the door.
- Is there someone you're connected to who has done something similar? What can you learn from them?
- What would make you confident enough to go for it?

The Sweet Spot of Goal Setting

As you lay out your new path and build it, step by step, remember to remain adaptable. "What we don't do enough of is implement triggers or checkpoints," Shoshanna Hecht said. "You want to start building some of that in. Otherwise you're going to keep being reactive. You'll live your life responding to email. You'll keep treating your inbox like a to-do list."

Hecht's "Have, Do, Be" framework guiding your decisions makes your roadmap easier to plot because your choices become more obvious. This is especially helpful if you're indecisive, as I am (seriously, where are my fellow Libras?)

During our first interview, Roshan Shah recalled a setback she experienced in 2015. While training for a half marathon, she fell off a treadmill. The injury cost her nearly two months of training, but she got back out there and began slowly running again as soon as she could. She ran the race she had set out to do. "I signed up with friends, and I felt an accountability to run it with them," she said. "It was really hard. It rained on us. I was crying and it was painful both during and after the race. I kept thinking, 'I'm physically fit enough that if I just try, no matter how slow I am, I'll get through this.'" And she did.

Almost a decade later, she's now training for another half marathon, which may sound masochistic, but Shah credits her determination to try it again to her experience getting through that race years ago. "I stumbled, I had the setback, but I survived and I did okay," she said. "And the feeling of accomplishment when I got to the end of it was truly gratifying."

Goal setting allows you to picture the moment you're working toward. It will fuel you to keep going. Breaking down the process of reaching that goal into small steps helps make the journey more enjoyable. It offers continuous satisfaction in reaching those small milestones before you reach the finish line, the same way checking things off a to-do list provides a sense of accomplishment.

"If I make the half marathon the goal, that's huge," she said. "And there's a lot of time between now and then. But if I make my next run the goal, then I'm embracing the process. That's how you get to the consistency."

That's when I told Shah about my word count spreadsheet. Writing a book is a huge and scary goal. My friend Aliza Licht, author of *Leave Your Mark* and *On Brand*, told me that committing to a certain number of words per day or per week makes the process much more manageable. She showed me her template for her word count spreadsheet that she used while writing both of her books, which I gratefully used as a model for my own.

One week in February, a month shy of my goal to have a completed first draft, I didn't meet my weekly word count goal. Inner critic Raz's raspy voice came roaring into my head that Friday, wondering why I was incapable of achieving the simple goal I set out for myself. But then I remembered Shah's advice, suggesting we all give ourselves more grace. So I did.

But the following week, I met and surpassed my word count goal. With a little practice, it's possible to retrain your thought process and turn self-doubt into motivation.

Let the Wall Crash Down

Amanda Goetz's marriage was falling apart. She knew her setback had been *Established*, but she wasn't sure what to do about it yet. So she found herself seeking anxiety relief in the form of alcohol overindulgence. But alcohol never really made her feel better. In fact, she started to notice that it heightened her anxiety. She needed to find another outlet. So she went into a spiral of research to find out why anxiety happens and alternative ways of addressing it.

That's how she came across the anxiety-reducing benefits of cannabidiol, more commonly known as CBD, the second most prevalent active ingredient in marijuana. She began reaching out to seed experts, growers, and others as she sought to learn more about the extraction process. She wanted to relieve her stress but she still associated cannabis with drug use, which did not appeal to her. Goetz was on a mission to understand how CBD could be effective without the bloodshot eyes and high associated with tetrahydrocannabinol (THC).

"This was in 2018," Goetz said. "It was starting to be legal, but hadn't really become mainstream yet. I went into wellness shops, the few dispensaries that had opened up, but all the products were very 'weed-themed.' I wanted to find something that would help calm my central nervous system but still allow me to do work and parent effectively."

As a first-generation college graduate from a town of eight hundred people in rural Illinois, Goetz was raised to focus on family and little else. She was engaged at nineteen and married at twenty-one. By the time she was thirty-two, she was the mother to three young children. A self-proclaimed "recovering Catholic," she had never touched cannabis. There was more of a stigma around drug use in her community than alcohol use. Because of her religious upbringing, she had also never considered that her marriage might be the thing causing her anxiety, or that divorce might be an option.

But as Goetz started working, first at Ernst & Young and then as a marketing executive leading a team of thirty at wedding website and marketplace The Knot, she realized she was actually pretty good at her career. When she looked at the dichotomy between her role at her job and her role as a wife, she began to notice that one was lighting her up much more than the other. She had gotten married at such a young age because of the expectations set out for her by her community, family, and friends, but she had never thought to question what she herself might want. As Goetz tiptoed into her setback, she froze around the decision to possibly leave her marriage. To avoid rumination, she sought therapy for the first time in her life. She stayed in Embrace for well over a year before she decided to move forward.

"Making a big decision when you're emotional is always a bad idea," she said. "I couldn't say 'I want a divorce' without crying. After six months of digging into the subconscious driver of all the decisions that led to this point, my next decision was clear. And I was finally able to say it without my voice shaking."

As she worked through Embrace, she cycled through a broad spectrum of emotions. Sometimes, her situation filled her with shame. But other times, it felt like an awakening, powering her desire to create a new life where she could be the driver of her own decisions, abandoning the expectations of those around her.

"Guilt is a huge part of my DNA," she said. "It was tough to break through a cloud of shame that I was not doing exactly what was taught to me, undoing the notion that this was the life I was supposed to have."

She could stay in her marriage and power through. She could continue to "it's fine" her way through the Setback Cycle. She could continue to maintain the status quo of her life that had been designed based on the plans of others. Or she could apply a growth mindset and figure out how to design her own life, on her own terms. She could leave her husband and create a new company based on the deep-rooted Curiosity she had begun exploring around anxiety relief. Of course, it would be harder, and she would have an uphill climb with plenty of obstacles in her way, but she could create something for the first time in her life that was truly hers.

As she confidently walked into Explore, she realized that deep-rooted Curiosity wasn't only about the world of CBD she was researching, but simultaneously about the life she might be able to create for herself and for others. It was scary. But it was exciting. She knew what she needed to do. So she asked her husband for a separation.

"My therapist pointed out that sometimes women are holding up a heavy wall that's falling down on them," Goetz continued. "When something gets heavier and heavier, you can't hold it up anymore. It eventually crushes you. But that's what women do—we try to hold everything up until it crushes us."

Starting over is scary until you make the leap. On the other side, most people question why they didn't take that leap sooner.

"Here's the thing," she whispered. "The wall is gone now. Once you let it all crash down, suddenly you look around and realize how much the room has opened up."

She filed for divorce when her youngest son was only eight weeks old. Goetz knew what she wanted to have, knew what she wanted to do, but needed to figure out how to become the person she actually wanted to *be* once that wall was gone. So with a suitcase, her three young kids, and the combination of fear and exhilaration over what would come next, she Emerged from her setback and walked into her new life.

Goetz was deeply inspired by the story of Brownie Wise. Credited with the rise of Tupperware parties, her unique approach to selling the product at gatherings in people's homes is what built the Tupperware brand into an empire.

But Wise was let go from the company in 1958. Her layoff was due to a tumultuous relationship with founder Earl Tupper, who resented the fame she had achieved. She was given one year's severance.

"Brownie Wise took her severance, went to Florida and lived a quiet life after Tupperware," Goetz said. "I named the company after her as a way to remind us to step into our power, to demand credit— and compensation—for what we've built, and to be as loud as we want about it."

House of Wise began as a cannabis company that focused on three critical needs—sex, stress relief, and sleep. When I asked Goetz why she chose those three to start with, she pointed out, "I just went through my day. What big things need to happen in order to have a good day? And what are the things I struggle with? It starts with sleep. If you don't have a good night's sleep, you're stressed the next day, and when you're stressed, your ability to regulate is harder."

So in order to have a good day, you also need to have sex? What mother of three is having sex every day? Seriously, though, please tell the rest of us all your secrets.

Goetz explained that the idea behind the product was more about embracing a woman's sexuality—especially moms, who are often told by society that their sexual desire is no longer important. Goetz also pointed out that you don't necessarily need a partner to have your sexual needs met—even on a daily basis. Plus, a very fun fact she shared—an orgasm triggers the body to release the hormone oxytocin, which reduces stress.

Despite emerging from the Setback Cycle with a new company and a renewed focus, as we know, the founder process is rife with many microsetbacks. The conversation around sexuality wasn't the only stigma Goetz was trying to break down. She quickly learned that even in 2019, before there was a dispensary on every corner of every major U.S. city, the stigma around cannabis put many obstacles in her way as she tried to create a business around it. She had trouble courting investors, getting banks to approve sales transactions, even getting social media platforms to approve her advertisements. She needed to continue using the small-step framework to work around the near-daily challenges that accompanied building a CBD business in the early days of the industry.

On the bright side, she really nailed the timing. Turns out, the world events of the past few years have really stressed people out. Many of us are full of anxiety, we are sleeping less, and having less sex. The cannabis industry remains one of the fastest growing industries in the U.S., expecting to reach $197 billion by 2028.[1]

Goetz also recognized that the cannabis industry is fraught with racial discrimination through the outsized criminalization of cannabis that disproportionately impacts people of color. That's why she partnered with an organization called Last Prisoner Project, a nonprofit committed to drug policy reform and freeing the estimated forty thousand prisoners incarcerated for cannabis in the U.S. House of Wise donated a portion of all proceeds to the organization's Family Support Fund, which benefits the children of those currently incarcerated.

Rethinking Work

While building House of Wise, Goetz became very vocal about how to optimize productivity while maintaining a healthy work-life balance, giving her employees flexible schedules and days off. She was a huge advocate of no-meeting Fridays. She pointed out that those of us who had made the shift to remote work, like me, were trying to be overly productive during our previous commuting times. And we were going to burn out. So she suggested an alternative: a "commute bath" every evening to decompress from the day and shift from work mode into (for her, personally) mom mode. Goetz wanted to make the most of every minute of her day—and that included prioritizing rest.

"I had four jobs in college. I know how to get a lot of shit done in a limited amount of time," Goetz said. "Most women do. Especially moms."

A single mom navigating entrepreneurship doesn't have time for inefficiency.

"I have navigated infertility, miscarriage, divorce, dating as a single mom, freezing my eggs, corporate jobs, my failed startup, the acquisition and merger of The Knot/Wedding Wire and am now navigating working from home and starting my own company in a pandemic with my kids full time," Goetz said to me over the phone just one month after House of Wise had officially launched in January 2021.

By removing unnecessary meetings and creating predictable work schedules that didn't fluctuate each week, Goetz was able to create space for the other areas and other roles in her employees' lives. In doing so, she was able to eliminate guilt around her employees having personal commitments. "It brought so much more joy and so much more productivity into people's lives," she said. "It's about quality over quantity. Care about the person behind the title. Go live your life and then come back. If one thing lights you up, you'll weave that into all the other parts of your life, including work."

Find the Berries

A setback is a moment when things don't go as expected. Amanda Goetz's setback prompted her to walk away from everything in her life that wasn't serving her—her marriage, her big corporate career. But as she started to build her company, she stepped into the unknown. She loved how rewarding it was to create something that had a real impact on improving people's lives. Through her products, the way she managed her team, and her approach to work structures, she found she was able to design systems that really altered people's lives. Her Plan B was taking shape as she entered a whole new field and connected with new communities. It was a drastic departure from her small-town upbringing, her role as a young wife and mother, and her early days in the corporate world. It was exhilarating, and a bit terrifying.

"Any new exploration is inherently dangerous, because you're in a place you don't know," said Chantel Prat. "Biologically, your brain is wondering, is this new neck of the woods more likely to get me eaten by a tiger? Or is this where I'll find the berries I'm looking for? Different brains have different ways of weighing costs and benefits, and if your brain decides that this place is worth exploring, it drives you to be brave and look for the good things."

If we could all just remember to look for the good things. To find the berries.

"If you are telling yourself that you are a failure or that setback is now linked to your identity, you will find mounting evidence that you suck," Prat said. "That's why sometimes our brains shut down as a form of self-preservation."

Shit. How do we prevent this?

"Have honest conversations with yourself," said Prat. "There's that knowing and doing gap. It's your brain's way of saying, are you really ready to get out there? Or do you need more time to process and heal? And if you identify as 'a failure,' how much evidence do you have that that story is true? Can you set that story aside and go look for alternate evidence?"

If we look back at the beginning of Goetz's story, it began with some of that self-exploration during therapy while she was still married. She was honest with herself, and despite feeling like a failure, she didn't just sit with the knowledge of what she should do, as so many of us do. She took action, rebuilt her life, and reaped all the rewards. She found the berries.

Emerging with an Exit

Several years after she launched House of Wise, Goetz took another dip in the S curve of her Setback Cycle as she chose to sell the company to new owners whom she saw as better equipped to scale it, redirecting the focus from direct-to-consumer to the many inbound retail partnerships that were driving most of her revenue. Goetz stayed on as an adviser and equity partner. She acknowledges how hard it was to exit the company she had worked so hard to build. The difficult choice came down to the fact that some of the growth of the business started coming from retailers. "We launched in Free People and saw a snowball effect of more and more inbound retail requests coming in," she said.

Goetz realized she needed to bring on leaders with skill sets that differed from her own in order to capitalize on these opportunities. "It came down to caring more about my customers than my ego," she says. "There were moments when people would tell me that House of Wise got them through something difficult like the passing of a loved one, a baby in a NICU, a breakup, menopause, you name it. Those are my biggest sources of pride and, ultimately, the reason I chose to exit the brand."

So what's next for Goetz? "My mission in life is to help women love themselves and make space for themselves," she said. "Whatever I continue to do, whether it's a passion project, a full-time gig, or something else, it will ladder up to that overall mission."

"Exiting the company in the way that I did is just a reminder that we have to stop thinking that there's only one way to do things," she continued. "Now I find myself in this narrative that my identity is a founder so I have to go build a multimillion-dollar brand. But maybe instead, I'll go live a quieter life."

Amanda Goetz Setback Cycle Snapshot

Phase 1: ESTABLISH	After getting married and having kids at a young age, Goetz found that her marriage was not lighting her up the way it used to.
Phase 2: EMBRACE	To work through it, she turned to therapy, as well as other coping tactics such as nightly glasses of wine. She wanted to climb out of rumination, exploring stress relief solutions that didn't involve the grogginess of alcohol, which is what led her to the cannabis industry. She harnessed a growth mindset and began learning about a nascent industry that still had a bit of stigma attached to it.
Phase 3: EXPLORE	Goetz continued working at her corporate job and building House of Wise on the side. As she explored her Curiosity, she navigated the obstacles of building a cannabis company early in the industry's nascency. This prompted her to tap into her superpowers of creativity and problem-solving. Entrepreneurship allowed her to pivot more easily, more frequently, and find new ways to approach work and team building.
Phase 4: EMERGE	She brought on investors, hired a team and created a model that helped women explore their stress, sleep and sexuality—destigmatizing the conversations around mothers and sexuality, the cannabis industry as a whole, and creating a successful, scalable business. After exiting House of Wise and selling it to another company, Goetz is now on to Plan C, which she is certain will involve helping women find new ways to prioritize themselves.

Goetz recognizes the pitfalls of getting too attached to one identity or place. She will always be a founder, whether she creates more businesses or not. But her skills are incredibly transferable and what she learned through her experiences can certainly benefit others. Now, she's doing marketing consulting while writing her newsletter, Life's A Game, about her ideas on how to create different approaches to work structures and systems. Whether she stays on with these gigs or not, her next move will undoubtedly serve to work toward that North Star.

There is no finish line. There is only evolution. Progress is nonlinear. But it's important to stop and recognize progress when we see it. Look at where you are now. Think back to a year ago. If you draw a line, can you see it? How have your goals shifted? How has your identity shifted? And when the time is right for your next pivot, will you be ready? How can you center your path forward around your personal North Star?

CHAPTER 10

Light the Way Forward

How are the world's best leaders able to get up every morning and make tough decisions? How does one dredge up the energy to work through the mundane daily tasks required to run a business? The answer is simple. They are all working toward a larger mission—their North Star. When one feels they are in service of an overall goal, it becomes easier to do the smaller, more tedious tasks that help them reach that goal.

Angela Duckworth notes in *Grit* that purpose is one of the strongest human motivators, even in the moments of mundanity.

"At its core, the idea of purpose is the idea that what we do matters to people other than ourselves," she says.[1] Many studies, from the National Institute of Health[2] to Pew Research,[3] have proven that leading a purpose-driven life correlates not only with success, but happiness and overall life satisfaction.

Finding Your North Star

Understanding your purpose, or your North Star, is a great tool that aids in decision-making, and perhaps more importantly, as many of us are pulled in way too many directions, boundary setting. Once you have your North Star crystalized, you can answer questions like do you need to go to that event? Respond to that email? Say yes to that coffee? What is worthy of your time and energy? And is it in service of that larger purpose?

In my marketing consulting, I frequently write brand and company mission statements. What if we did that exercise for ourselves? It's time to clarify your purpose, identify your North Star, and distill it into your own personal mission statement.

Writing Your Personal Mission Statement

1. Identify your values. Write them down.
2. What emotional benefits do you offer to those around you?
3. What functional benefits do you offer?
4. What are three to five of your attributes?
5. What are your goals? They can be career goals, business goals, and/or personal goals. Pick one to three and write them down.

Read your answers to the above. Make connections, prioritize the most important pieces, consolidate, and condense into one or two sentences to summarize and clarify your personal mission statement.

If you read through that list and thought, "I don't have functional benefits," think of the role you play in group dynamics. Are you the one making restaurant reservations, scheduling time with your friends, doing the grocery shopping in your household, cooking meals, feeding your family? The functional benefits outlined here range from scheduling to logistics, to meeting the fundamental human need of food and drink. When's the last time you showed someone kindness? The emotional benefits of that gift, that favor, the thank-you note? You made someone feel appreciated, welcome, seen. Those are some strong emotional benefits and they can be achieved by the smallest acts. Add it to your mission statement. See how it matches up with some of your other answers.

"People will say things like, 'I don't have time to come up with a mission statement,'" Shoshanna Hecht pointed out, "but having something like that is exactly the thing they need to help them stay focused on the task at hand. It really does speak to what can happen when you can see a path forward."

What's your inner critic's name again? Give them a quick nod of acknowledgement and ask them to quiet down for the moment. Ol' Raz is being quiet right now so I'll share my answers to this exercise:

My emotional benefits include enabling others to feel seen, heard and celebrated. The functional benefits I offer are to inform, inspire, and uplift. My attributes are strength, energy, integrity, and connections-making. My goals are to tell stories, have fun, support my community, and celebrate those around me.

All this leads into my own mission statement:

My purpose is to tell the stories of those making a positive impact on their communities, and in doing so, inspire others to realize they too can make a significant impact on those around them.

If I look back at where I focused my efforts throughout my life, this North Star has always been there. From volunteering in my early twenties to my early-aughts travel blog, telling the stories of community-driven leadership has been a constant. I didn't identify that until years later. But maybe you can find yours earlier than I did if you write out your mission statement now. The connections will be there and they'll become clearer as you become more tuned into it.

Perhaps a few years from now, or a few setbacks from now, I'll adjust my mission statement. That's okay. Your purpose should evolve, or come a bit more into focus, as you move through the different seasons of your life.

Luminary Leadership

Luminary founder Cate Luzio has always been driven by her purpose, and she brings her vision to life through perseverance, grit, and determination. It's what motivated her to leave banking and create a professional education and networking platform to help women succeed in their careers, across all industries and sectors. Guided by that mission, Luzio is able to evaluate the many decisions a business owner like her is faced with every single day, feeling confident that everything she does is in service of her North Star.

Growing up as the middle child sandwiched between two brothers, Luzio always felt like the only girl in the room. In fact, she was the only girl on her entire block, something Luzio saw as an advantage. She started playing sports at a young age, which she attributes to her early sense of leadership, community, and team building. Her father taught her the value of perseverance. "My father made sure I understood that when I fell down, I needed to get back up and walk it off," Luzio said. "He made it clear that we had to work really hard and nothing would be handed to us. We were very bluntly told that if we wanted something, we needed to go after it."

That experience served her well through her nearly two-decade banking career. As Luzio drew on her confidence and worked to hold her own among various groups of overconfident alpha personalities, she noticed that other women weren't nearly as comfortable as she was in male-dominated environments. As a result, they weren't developing the type of camaraderie Luzio had with her colleagues. The doors held open for her were closed for some of her peers. Luzio leaned into that "walk it off" mantra, feeling lucky in terms of how her upbringing helped her find success. She wanted to share what she had learned with the women around her. "It's what lit up this passion and purpose inside me," she said.

Luzio also had a gut instinct that the polite office conversations and the coffee chats with her colleagues were barely scratching the surface of something deeper.

That's why she created a monthly dinner series, aptly named The Whisper Network, where her peers could talk openly about what they were experiencing in their workplaces.[4] It was in these smaller, intimate circles where they finally felt comfortable candidly sharing the challenges they faced. Conversations ranged from how to handle compensation inequality, denial of new opportunities, and retaliation for sharing honest feedback. It was also an opportunity to make new connections. Luzio saw an urgent need to create a forum for sharing, figure out solutions to pressing issues, and help her peers feel more supported.

Tuning into the needs of her community is something Luzio has always been good at. It's one of her superpowers.

She knew there was more she could be doing than just this monthly dinner series. Her tipping point arrived when one of her mentors asked, "What do you want to do with the rest of your career?" Luzio knew that her future wasn't going to be stepping into the role of CEO at a financial institution. It was a coveted title she could have worked toward, but she knew deep down it wasn't what she wanted. She drew on her fearlessness around the unknown, applied a growth mindset, and decided it was time to try something new. So, after almost twenty years in banking, she left the industry.

Faced with a wave of uncertainty after climbing the corporate ladder in one industry for most of her career, how could she even fathom where to turn next? Had she made a mistake in leaving her lucrative career and comfortable position? Sometimes a setback is one we willfully walk into. Is that what she had done? Was leaving banking a terrible mistake?

Luzio was working through the Setback Cycle to figure out her next move. As she cycled through Embrace, she reflected on what she was most proud of when she looked back on her long career: the women's programs she created at the organizations she worked at, the connections she created for others, the client and peer relationships, and the ability to lead and develop talent while building thriving businesses for three of the largest banks in the world. She was at her best when she was mentoring, managing, and helping women uplevel the skills they had often been socialized to avoid, such as negotiating and advocating for themselves.

As she got to the Explore phase, she turned toward her deep-rooted Curiosity, remembering how much she loved being part of a team, especially as a kid playing sports. She leaned into her superpowers of cultivating community, just as she had with The Whisper Network. Once she got to Emerge, she was clear on her North Star. It was time to use the small-step decision-making framework to plot her next move.

Three weeks after she walked away from her banking career, the business plan for Luminary was complete. Eight months later, in November 2018, the physical space opened its doors in New York City's NoMad (short for "north of Madison Square Park") neighborhood, boasting sweeping views of the city.

Luminary can mean a guiding light, an inspiration, a role model, a heroine, a leader, or a legend. And that's exactly the role Luzio hoped her new company would play. Luzio's mission was to reach women across the board, from rising executives, to founders, to those at a crossroads, and more. She hoped to create something that catered to everyone at every stage in their career. Soon, she was hosting workshops, events, panels, and educational talks. From the individual memberships to the programs she created for her corporate partners, Luzio's vision for Luminary was (and still is) the ultimate advocate for women of all ages, through all the seasons of their careers—and lives.

By 2019, that vision was coming to life in ways that exceeded her wildest expectations.

"I got the sense that Luminary's community is a large draw," *Business Insider's* Melissa Wiley wrote. "I noticed women of all ages entering the space. Many people greeted each other by name. Male allies were welcome as well."[5]

Luzio was careful to create a description of Luminary that focused on both professional and personal growth. For example, early events ranged from Business Plan Boot Camp to The Key to Your Thriving Business Starts with Your Well-Being. The speakers for these workshops and events ranged from successful founders to recruiters and executives from behemoth organizations like J.P. Morgan and Unilever, two of Luminary's corporate partners. Luminary also offered casual happy hours, new member breakfasts and mixers for founders, moms, and others who were seeking community.

Luzio could always plan ahead while understanding it was impossible to predict the unpredictable. What she truly never could have predicted was how much she would have to rely on this strength to get through one of the toughest periods of her career.

The Glorified #GirlBoss Era

Around the same time Luzio was beginning to create her plans for Luminary, women's coworking spaces were starting to become more and more common. The timing made sense, following the post-2016 election era of feminism, preceded by years of women founders trying to build their businesses in male-dominated environments that didn't feel super welcoming. In response, a crop of new spaces catered toward a new generation of women founders cropped up. It's time to talk about the era of the #girlboss. Grab an oat milk latte and settle in.

This movement was created in response to the bro culture at WeWork–style coworking spaces across the country. Women entrepreneurs wanted to build their businesses in safe, comfortable women-centric spaces, which is what paved the way for The Wing, The Riveter, Chief, Luminary, and more, all of which opened between 2017 and 2019.

These community and collaboration spaces weren't just for founders. I remember being drawn to The Wing's shiny, pink Millennial feminist vibe with conference room names like Gloria Steinem and Fran Fine (Fran Drescher's character from *The Nanny*.) Even though the company where I worked had a lovely office in midtown,

The Wing offered a space where I could take my coworkers to collaborate on projects, get some work done, have coffee, share overpriced avocado toast, and plot what we saw as world domination.

It also offered a beautiful pumping room. After returning from maternity leave in early 2019, I spent three, sometimes four separate twenty-minute periods each day sitting in a glorified closet as I expressed food for my new baby out of my body. The pumping room at my office was a windowless room, furnished with two small chairs, a refrigerator for storage, and nothing else as it was the size of a small closet. Meanwhile, there were often two, sometimes three of us crammed in there at once trying to pump, email and take conference calls. There was no semblance of privacy in that shared space. But The Wing's vast, velvet-curtained, large pink armchair–filled spacious pumping room with all the supplies a new mom could ever dream of was one of the biggest draws at the time. Apparently, when you become a mother your idea of a good time shifts from booze and bars to avocado toast and breastmilk. Coffee, avocado toast, pump, repeat.

This was all in the heyday of The Wing, well before the company experienced a widely publicized takedown when accusations of their founder, who built a brand based on inclusion, was supposedly mistreating her own employees. Her downfall came alongside those of numerous women founders, from Away's Steph Korey to Glossier's Emily Weiss to the Chief founders. Despite the varying details of each situation, which honestly, the public will never fully know, the one constant was that these founders were undoubtedly held to much higher standards than their tech bro counterparts.

As Leslie Feinzaig put it in her *Fast Company* article about female founder takedowns, "Those women who do break through and achieve a modicum of success, against the odds, inevitably grow a target on their back. Because when a woman succeeds, too many people— including other women—resent her for it. And for ambitious female founders of high growth companies, all too often success leads to a takedown."[6]

Many of the founders I've interviewed will tell you all about the delicate dance they do trying to run a profitable business while being as morally sound and gracious as possible—a standard that rarely seems to matter for the other 97 percent of venture capital-backed founders—men.

As the rah-rah #girlboss movement morphed into what felt like a weekly series of "Who's next?" women founder takedowns, the pandemic hit. As offices shut down, so did coworking spaces. With economic uncertainty looming, memberships went on pause indefinitely. Would any of these spaces survive?

In February 2020, Luminary was celebrating a successful first year in business, having hosted over two hundred in-person events, a steadily growing membership, and a new addition that Luzio was giddily excited about—a rooftop bar and restaurant appropriately named The Glass Ceiling just above the existing space.

That month, Luzio hosted a press dinner on that rooftop. Buzz was swirling, projections were great, and she was feeling confident that the momentum of the past year had pushed Luminary forward as a category leader.

On March 11, Luzio was dashing between various Women's History Month speaking engagements around the city. She got a text from a Luminary member who was in China at the time. It read, "Things are worse than you think, be prepared."

Luzio remembers laughing.

The member responded, "I'll send masks."

The next day, the World Health Organization declared Covid-19 a pandemic. New York City shut down along with the rest of the world. In-person events were canceled. Luzio and her team scrambled frantically to move all of Luminary's scheduled March events from in-person to virtual.

Confident humility is one of Luzio's biggest strengths. That means she has complete confidence in what she's capable of, but she also acknowledges when there's something she's not an expert in, which enables her to enlist the advice of those around her and remain open to adapting when necessary. She relied on her team to help her make the pivot to digital, and she turned to her community—the Luminary members—to figure out what they needed most at this time.

"Harness the benefits of doubt," Adam Grant says, guiding us on how to find confident humility.[7] "You can have confidence in your capacity to learn while questioning your current solution to a problem. Knowing what you don't know is often the first step toward developing expertise."

During this setback, Luzio was sure of one thing—her North Star. Her determination to stay true to her mission of helping women navigate career transitions. If there was ever a time to show up for her community, she knew this was it.

Luminary's first digital event was called Don't Touch Your Face, Don't Touch Your 401k.

The next morning, Luzio woke up with a dry cough. She didn't think much of it. Then, as she stepped into the shower, she opened up her bottle of face wash. It was the one she loved so much because the smell reminded her of her grandmother. Luzio was alarmed when she realized she couldn't smell it. In fact, she couldn't smell anything. She started opening everything she could reach, shampoos, soaps, toothpaste. Luzio frantically threw a towel on and ran into her bedroom where her boyfriend was sitting on a Zoom call with his entire company. In a panic, he excused himself from his meeting and went into the kitchen, retrieving a bottle of everything bagel seasoning. Luzio smelled it. Nothing.

She cleared her throat to speak, but at that moment, as with anyone who contracted Covid in the early days of March 2020, the only words she could muster were, "Oh, fuck."

Luzio was determined not to fail her community in those early days. No newcomer to the Setback Cycle, she was cycling through Embrace once again, but she didn't have time to pause. They were virtual anyway at this point, so what was the harm in working through her illness? She did virtual appointments with her doctor, who advised her not to go to a hospital or to any in-person doctor's office since they were overwhelmed with patients. Luzio became comfortable pushing that mute button on calls as her cough persisted. She led events and workshops and participated in press interviews, making sure to let everyone in her community know she was still there for them.

Still, people were in panic mode. They put their memberships on hold. Luminary lost 80 percent of its revenue in those first two months. Luzio was forced to accept her reality, as there was no way to "it's fine" her way through this. So she remained laser focused on her community, regularly updating and checking in on Luminary members and staff. Meanwhile, she was now battling a case of long Covid. The lack of rest had caught up with her. She was sick and she was scared.

One day, she called a Zoom meeting, looking at the boxes on the screen with the faces of her trusted teammates, who were also working long hours to get through this impossible time. She presented the options. "Look," she told them, "Things aren't looking good. We could do layoffs, furloughs, or pay cuts." She told them to take their time and think about it. But they didn't need to. At that moment, one by one, every single employee spoke up, asking for a pay cut so they could remain a part of the team, continue building their vision of what Luminary could be, together, without losing any of their valued colleagues.

Inspired by her own staff's camaraderie, loyalty, and resilience, Luzio doubled down on her commitment to her North Star. She was going to do everything in her power to keep her community afloat.

Luzio moved into Explore. She needed answers, and she knew she could find them if she had the right information. She tapped into that Curiosity she knew well, using confident humility to make sure she could get to the answers she wasn't pretending to have yet. Luzio started gathering information, spending those early days on the phone with her accountant, her landlord, and everyone she worked with to make sure the business she had left her comfortable banking job to build from scratch wouldn't fall apart only one year in.

When Luzio thinks back to that time, she remembers trying to figure out how what she built could continue to serve the careers, businesses and lives of professional women. "I don't care if five people or 500 people show up to an event, whether in person or virtual," she said. "If five people walk away with advice, a connection or two, some resources, something that inspires them, that, to me, is success."

From the Shecession to the Great Resignation

Several months into the pandemic, society began to experience what was dubbed the "shecession," which economists called a once-in-a-generation mass exodus of women from the workforce. This was partially due to caregivers struggling to balance the lack of childcare and remote schooling, and partially due to women having more time to consider why they were spending all their time and energy at workplaces that didn't really value them. Luzio thought back to her Whisper Network days. It seemed like those whispers had turned into screams. In fact, the *New York Times* set up a hotline where parents could call to let out a primal scream and vent about the impossibility of balancing work and parenting.

Meanwhile, leadership teams and HR departments were also scrambling. They wanted to figure out how to prevent some of their best talent from leaving. And who better positioned to help them navigate this period than Luzio—someone with experience in the corporate world who had always had her finger on the pulse of what women really needed to succeed. She could certainly counsel large organizations through this moment. She was finally cycling into Emerge.

It was time to run through the small-step framework again, going through the same process that led her to create Luminary after leaving her banking career. How could she scale up her offerings for these organizations in a meaningful way? Before the pandemic, Luminary had a handful of corporate partners who offered memberships to NYC-area employees. But now all programming was digital, so the opportunities to expand these memberships was now global. Luzio saw an opportunity to stay true to her original mission while recouping lost revenue. She drew on her own experience in the corporate world and enlisted executive coaches to create programming tailored to retaining talented women at these organizations. Sure, Luzio cared about impact, but impact at scale, especially during a time when so many women were struggling, could be game changing. And she also wasn't excluding men. Being able to offer something truly inclusive while staying focused on her mission enabled her to stand out from other women's membership organizations and career development platforms.

Luzio brought on twelve additional corporate partners in late 2020. While the corporate partnerships were critical, more than 70 percent of Luminary's programming remained tailored toward individual members. She also launched a fellowship program to support women and women business owners impacted by the pandemic in late 2020. Those programs have supported over two thousand women to date. Now, over ten thousand members in thirty-six countries have access to Luminary's coaching, training, events, and community.

Two years later, Luminary membership quadrupled organically, meaning without any paid advertising or membership recruiting efforts, an industry anomaly. Luzio had not only come back from that initial 80 percent revenue dip, she more than soared past it.

When the world began to open back up in 2022, Luzio took Luminary to dozens of cities to help struggling coworking spaces around the country. She built a permanent on-the-road experience across multiple cities, now called Luminary LIVE, further expanding that community she so carefully created.

Eventually, the five million women who exited the workforce in 2020 as part of the Shecession movement started to return. Companies began to ask employees to come back to their offices, which was welcomed by some, rejected by many. As these complicated "return to office" conversations took off, Luzio helped steer those discussions, not just with employees and founders, but also with her corporate partners. To her, transparent conversation could lead to thoughtful solutions.

As the workplace continued to shift over the next few years, Luzio accurately predicted that the Great Resignation (the economic trend that led employees to voluntarily resign from their jobs en masse due to limited career advancement opportunities, hostile work environments, job dissatisfaction, and more)[8] would morph into a recession. Faced with an uncertain economy, large companies began a slew of mass layoffs. And once again, Luzio collaborated with her team to discuss what professional women needed at this moment. Did they want to find new jobs or try to freelance? If they kept their jobs, did they want to return to the office or continue working remotely? Did they risk proximity bias if they refused to go back? Of course, the answer was different depending on the individual circumstances. Luminary guided these discussions with individuals and with organizations, once again supporting the evolving needs of women in the workforce, even as those needs continue to shift.

Now Luminary is thriving online, across the country, and at the original space in New York City. As I sit here, writing this manuscript on a Thursday afternoon in 2023 waiting for an event to begin, the space is once again filled with people, bustling with energy, and humming with excitement.

Every time I talk to Luzio, I'm convinced she is made of Teflon. No stranger to setbacks, she remains adaptable, truly listening to understand the evolving needs of her community. She can predict cultural trends but doesn't get caught up in fleeting ones, and is able to acknowledge when it's time for a pivot. Her bullshit filter is A+. Through it all, she remains committed to her North Star, the same thing that inspired her to create The Whisper Network, and later, Luminary—her mission of supporting the evolving needs of women throughout their career journeys.

Cate Luzio Setback Cycle Snapshot

Phase 1: ESTABLISH	After creating Luminary, a space for women at all stages of their career, and seeing a successful first year, Luzio's space was forced to close due to the onset of the pandemic and the stay-at-home orders. People began canceling memberships, unsure about what the future might hold.
Phase 2: EMBRACE	Luzio didn't have time to "it's fine" everything away or deny that she was in a setback. She has always been a realist and a woman of action. She sat in her setback as she worked to address the logistics of her situation. As she battled an early and severe case of Covid, she kept going, even when she perhaps should have rested.
Phase 3: EXPLORE	Drawing on her superpower of confident humility and tapping into her constellation, she enlisted her team to make collective decisions, even when those decisions were extremely tough. As she slowly steered her business forward, she recognized the enormous impact she would still be able to have on women at all stages of their careers all over the world.
Phase 4: EMERGE	Her corporate partners grew concerned about retaining women as they fled the workforce. Luminary was perfectly situated to help. It was time to run through the small-step framework again, going through the same process that led her to create Luminary after leaving her banking career. She did the same to help her partners navigate the next few workplace movements, from the Great Resignation to the recession to the return to office debates. Luzio Emerged from her setback by expanding her reach, and her impact. Two years later, Luminary had expanded to twelve corporate partners and over ten thousand members worldwide.

"I'll never forget that it was the Luminary community who rallied early on in the pandemic when we had to temporarily close our doors and put all programming online," Luzio wrote in one of her widely shared LinkedIn posts. "Right now, as each week brings news of economic tumult and layoffs, many people in your network might be struggling. Consider how you might be able to reach out and help."[9]

Despite the demise of the "Girl Boss" era and the decline in women's coworking and collaboration spaces, hers is still standing. And as she continues to expand her constellation, she's working to help others remain standing as well.

Find your North Star. Decide not only what you want to *have* and what you want to *do*, but whom you want to *be* as you look ahead and plot your path forward. You have cycled through some squiggly S shapes and emerged with resilience, strength, and a clear sense of self. Your metamorphosis is complete. You're ready for your Creative rebirth.

CONCLUSION

Creative Rebirth

It's rare that one can realize the transformation they are about to embark on the moment their world falls apart, or in my own very technical term, that "oh, fuck" moment. It's easy to see clearly with the advantage of hindsight. But I'm hopeful that after reading this book, you Emerge with the understanding that while setbacks are inevitable and some are way more significant than others, there's a cycle you can work your way through to get to the other side of that squishy, squiggly S.

Emerging from a setback feels victorious. Disruption leads to transformation. Posttraumatic growth is based on the evidence that we can come out stronger and find more meaning in our lives after going through dark times. Bottoming out often leads to a new beginning.

"I wish we didn't have to hit rock bottom," said Roshan Shah. "But sometimes that's the sort of catalyst we need to propel us forward. Feeling like you have nothing left to lose offers you the opportunity to take a bigger risk."

Creative rebirth doesn't always have to come from pain. "Not every difficult experience is trauma," said Adam Grant in a widely shared Instagram post. "Not every upsetting event is harm…. Confusing life-altering pain with discomfort minimizes suffering and undermines resilience."[1]

Setbacks aren't always traumatic. They range from the subtle everyday microsetbacks to the major, head-bonking, life-changing ones. Perhaps you accidentally tiptoed into one; perhaps you were dealt a difficult hand. Sometimes we realize it in the moment; sometimes we get there following years of reflection. Now we have the tools to recognize it when it happens so we can avoid sleepwalking into setbacks. Most important is what we do with that realization next time we find ourselves embarking on the Setback Cycle.

"We know that we have to get out of reactivity, but it's so easy to stay," Shoshanna Hecht said. "It's so easy to float along. It's hard to change."

Dr. Michelle Casarella agreed. "Some people are scared of failure, but others can be scared of success," she said.

Dr. Casarella shared a story about a friend from graduate school who became ABD, which stands for "all but dissertation." Graduate school at the doctoral level consists of coursework, internships, and a dissertation that all factor into the student's ability to graduate. You can go through years of schooling, but if you don't finish your dissertation, you don't get your doctorate.

Dr. Casarella's friend fell into that category. She was scared of success. She already had children and until now, her husband had been the primary household breadwinner. She was afraid of those roles shifting. Some people's fear of success is rooted in their fear of a changing relationship dynamic.

There's one last question you can consider if by now, there's any lingering hesitation in how to move forward.

"What do you want people to say about you at your funeral?" Dr. Casarella suggests asking. "Get specific though. Go beyond 'beloved spouse, parent, child, etc.' Even writing down a list of adjectives will be helpful."

It's like the reverse of "Have, Do, Be."

Did you *get* it?

Did you *do* it?

Did you become the person you want to *be*?

What is the legacy you'll leave behind?

I started writing this book seven months after my sister-in-law passed away. The birth of our children so close together strengthened the connection I shared with Erika. The bonds of motherhood were even tighter than the one we already shared as two women married into the same family. The sister-in-law dynamic is one that's not talked about nearly enough. If you're lucky enough to find a good one, hold tight and nurture that relationship. We frequently texted about sleep training, milk supply, in-law dynamics, and coordinating family holidays. She was taken away just as our relationship was evolving into something bigger, something we were never fully able to explore. I was so anxious about that family trip to Belize. I could not be more grateful that we went. We made plans for the summer as we said goodbye at the airport. It was the last time I ever saw her.

As we concluded her memorial ceremony on that crisp fall day, my brother-in-law encouraged us all to do one thing that afternoon. To try to *do* something Erika would have done. To try and *be* a little more like Erika. As we scattered wildflower seeds around the park, there were no questions about what those instructions meant. We knew what her North Star was. She was an incredible mother to her two young children, a dedicated wife and daughter, a loving sister and aunt, and a fantastic sister-in-law. She worked at the Environmental Protection Agency (EPA) for years. But none of those things alone defined her.

We knew who she was outside of all those qualifiers. At that ceremony, he was asking us all to be kinder, more caring—of the environment, of our communities, of our families, of each other. We were all clear on who she was. The instructions to *be* meant to be considerate. To foster meaningful relationships with those around us. To plant butterfly flowers in our gardens, as she had in her front yard. To pause and look around. To stop rushing. To appreciate our surroundings. To be more thoughtful. To be like Erika. To just *be*.

Climbing Out of the Gray Space

As society collectively emerges from what feels like a series of massive setbacks over the past few years, perhaps we can collectively forge that path forward together. We saw what these inspirational leaders and innovators did to work through their setbacks, and now you have the framework to not only guide you through yours, but to remind you that you can do the same.

Perhaps the next time you hear your alarm clock going off and *Establish* that you're in a setback, you'll *Embrace* your "oh, fuck" moment, consider an expectations audit as you avoid the slippery slope of reflection to rumination so you can thaw yourself out from the freeze. Befriend the asshole in your head, but quiet her when she gets loud so you can adopt a growth mindset. Figure out what truly drives you as you *Explore* your choices, cultivate your Curiosity, identify your superpowers, and build your community. You'll use your mission statement to help you connect with your North Star and scenario plan to propel you forward as you *Emerge* to reveal what more might be possible.

"Disruptive times really open the door for new ideas," fashion designer Norma Kamali said in our interview. "It inspires creativity. So if you've got an idea, do it and do it boldly, fearlessly and give it your all. If it doesn't work, I promise you'll come out of the experience so empowered and so aware of what you're capable of."

We will all float along at some point. We may even sleepwalk into inevitable setbacks. We will definitely make more mistakes. But we might be more likely to admit when we are wrong. And we may even find a bit of joy in the experience as we move closer to getting things right.

No, everything does not happen for a reason. But things happen. How will you approach your next setback?

Enable the evolution to happen. Identify the phase of the cycle you're in. Let go of old expectations, sever your "shoulds," take what you learn, remain flexible, and adapt.

These are the stories of the everyday trailblazers who have proven that setbacks can lead to something better. That failure can lead to flourishing. They're still working to create that better world—for the benefit of all.

Reshma Saujani continues her childcare advocacy efforts, trying to bridge support from the government and the private sector. She launched the National Business Coalition for Childcare and continues to have conversations with senior White House officials to make the economic case for expanding care in America. [2]

Amanda Goetz is traveling the world and taking on exciting new projects as she figures out what her life, and career, look like after selling House of Wise.

Palak Patel's cookbook comes out next month as she looks to expand her Atlanta restaurant to a larger space.

Stacy London finally sold her TV series idea about women in midlife.

Blessing Adesiyan is writing her own book about how to build a workplace that truly supports caregivers as she continues to expand Mother Honestly, now called MH WorkLife.

Cyrus Veyssi was recently featured in campaigns for Dior, MAC and Neutrogena. They continue to post about their loving and supportive relationship with their baba, who is also now beloved by fans around the world.

So, reader, what about you? You now have a fresh piece of paper, a blank canvas. What's your next chapter? Where will the cycle lead you next?

APPENDIX

The Setback Cycle Workbook

Phases and Concepts

Establish

- Alarm Clock Checklist

Embrace
- Thaw Yourself Out
- Expectations Audit

Explore
- The Curiosity Quiz
- Identify Your Superpower
- Connect with Your Constellation

Emerge
- Scenario Planning
- Decision-Making Framework
- Your North Star/Mission Statement

Activity Recap

PHASE ONE: ESTABLISH

Alarm Clock Checklist

- Every day (or a minimum of three days a week if every day is not possible,) rate your motivation on a scale of one to ten.
- Now rate your mood (happy, sad, angry, burned out, languishing, bored, etc.).
- List your activities for the day.
- Draw any obvious connections you see on one given day.

After a month, look back on your motivation scale and your mood ratings. Now see if you can draw patterns based on what activities surround any low scores. For your mood, see what words pop up most frequently.

Next, ask yourself the following questions:

- What are you most energized by?
- What are you disengaged with?
- Are you where you are because of a conscious decision to be there, or because of inertia?
- Are there any common themes that seem to be causing you undue stress?
- What can you acknowledge even if you can't act on it or solve it right now?

PHASE TWO: EMBRACE

> **Thaw Yourself Out**
>
> If you're still stuck in a freeze, focused on the pain or disappointment of what you're going through, consider the following questions:
>
> - Did it teach you something about what you want and don't want in your life?
> - Did it teach you some positive things that you might want to apply to future relationships?
> - Are you blaming someone else for this? Can you forgive that person and wish them well?
> - Are you blaming yourself? Can you give yourself a little more grace?
> - What have you learned? What new information do you have?

> **Expectations Audit** (by Morra Aarons-Mele)[3]
>
> Start this exercise by asking:
>
> - What drives you? Is it your own expectations, or the expectations of others?
> - Are those expectations crushing you, making every day harder?
>
> If your expectations feel overwhelming, consider setting aside five minutes to write down the following:
>
> - A big milestone you've reached, or one you're currently working toward. It could be a specific job title, a completed project, a business goal, a salary figure, a fitness goal, or any marker of progress and accomplishment.
> - If it's your own expectation, take a look at it again. What might you change?
> - Ask: Is this an expectation I want to keep? Or can I let this one go?

PHASE THREE: EXPLORE

The Curiosity Quiz

Get to Know Idealist You

Think back to your childhood, or your early, idealistic years, whenever those years may have been.

- What are you doing when you feel most like yourself?
- Where do you retreat when you want to escape or relax?
- What's the one hobby you've always enjoyed above everything else, or the one thing in life you've loved since you were little?
- What did you enjoy doing as a kid? Did you play an instrument? Do team sports? Read under a tree?
- What was exciting and fun about doing those activities? What did you love about them?

Introduce Idealist You to Realist You

- Who are you now? Don't say what your job is—in one sentence, write down who you are, as a person. How would your best friend describe you?
- If you stare out the window for five minutes and let your mind wander, where does it go? If you haven't allowed yourself to daydream in a while, go ahead. Where do those dreams take you?
- If money weren't a factor and you could have any job you wanted, what would you do?
- What is fear preventing you from doing?
- How could you take one small baby step toward doing that thing you're afraid of?

Identify Your Superpower

- What have people told you you're amazing at?
- What feels effortless to you that others struggle with?
- What do people learn when they first meet you?
- What do you see more clearly than others?
- What do people say when they brag about you?
- In a work setting, what would fall apart if you were to leave?

Connect with Your Constellation

How do you start making those deeper connections? Instead of asking, "What do you do?" when you first meet a person, McPherson suggests starting with one of the following. It also helps to have these prompts handy if you find yourself in an awkward pause in conversation:

- How are you spending your time these days?
- If you could be anywhere in the world next week, where would it be and why?
- What was your favorite food as a child? (You get so much more than naming a dish out of this question!)
- What was the last best podcast you listened to?
- If you were going to solve one world problem, and money wasn't an issue, what would it be?

PHASE FOUR: EMERGE

Scenario Planning: The ABC Approach

- Plan A is the *Ideal Plan*—the ideal outcome you want to experience.
- Plan B is the *Backup Plan*—when you can't achieve Plan A, how can you refocus to achieve something that is more attainable and still valuable?
- Plan C is the *Safety Net* (or backup to the backup)—if neither the A nor B plan is achieved, this changes the focus again so you can still achieve something meaningful.

Small-Step Decision-Making Framework
Have + Do + Be
1. In five years, what do you want to have?
2. What do you want to be doing? How do you want to be spending most of your time?
3. In five years, who will you be?

Now let's get granular. Write out a big goal. Then break it down into smaller, more manageable steps. If this goal is something like launching your own business, what are the twenty steps you need to take to get there? Start to consider the details.

- What resources will you need to get started on day one?
- If you need to leave a job in order to start that business, list out the things you need in order to confidently walk out the door.
- Is there someone you're connected to who has done something similar? What can you learn from them?
- What would make you confident enough to go for it?

Writing Your Personal Mission Statement
1. Identify your values. Write them down.
2. What emotional benefits do you offer to those around you?
3. What functional benefits do you offer?
4. What are three to five of your attributes?
5. What are your goals? They can be career goals, business goals, and/or personal goals. Pick one to three and write them down.

Read your answers to the above. Make connections, prioritize, consolidate, and condense into one or two sentences to summarize and clarify your personal mission statement.

Cycle Summaries

Reshma Saujani Setback Cycle Snapshot

Phase 1: ESTABLISH	Over a decade following Saujani's public setback that led her to create Girls Who Code, she, along with every parent she knew, experienced firsthand the struggle of trying to balance her own job with remote school and a lack of childcare.
Phase 2: EMBRACE	Saujani waited for what she felt would be an inevitable plan someone must be working on to help struggling parents. After adequate reflection, she wondered why society seemed to be ignoring the struggles of parents, from those who worked outside the home to those who were sole caregivers, undervalued and undercompensated.
Phase 3: EXPLORE	Saujani realized no relief was coming. If someone was going to come up with a plan, she would have to do it herself. She researched previous economic relief plans and recovery packages. Eventually, Saujani decided to tap into her innate superpower of taking a situation by the reins and getting shit done, her efforts now aimed at solving this glaring societal issue.
Phase 4: EMERGE	Saujani drafted an outline for what would soon be known as the Marshall Plan for Moms, a postpandemic recovery framework that offered relief for working parents, and compensation to parents whose labor was previously unpaid. She started to see a snowball effect as she had conversations with local and state governments, even seeing some success at the federal level.

My Setback Cycle Snapshot

Phase 1: ESTABLISH	I came back to work as a new mom, struggling to find balance and navigate a new identity. Confused about where to direct my energy, at home, at work, or some combination of both, I allowed myself to float along, convincing myself everything was fine and pretending I wasn't struggling to find my place.
Phase 2: EMBRACE	It eventually became clear that I needed to stop ignoring my discomfort. It didn't matter why, or how it was happening, I was stuck in a freeze and needed to find a way to thaw out.
Phase 3: EXPLORE	I looked around my workplace to find new opportunities and turned, as I always did, to writing. The answers, for me, often revealed themselves on the page.
Phase 4: EMERGE	In retrospect, I realized my internal alarm clock had been ringing for quite some time. It took years, but I found a way to feel valued again—this time, not so much from external validation but within myself. It came from exploring passions outside of the day job I had previously given everything to. I somehow found a healthy balance between motherhood, working, and writing on the side. I reflected on my setback journey. I started seeing the stories of setbacks in the journeys of all the founders and leaders I interviewed. I began talking to experts about this phenomenon. I wrote this book.

Amy Nelson Setback Cycle Snapshot

Phase 1: ESTABLISH	As Nelson tries to salvage her shattered company in the wake of the pandemic, armed FBI agents knock on her door, enter her home, accuse her husband of a crime, and seize all her family's assets. This defining moment signals a significant setback for Nelson and her family.
Phase 2: EMBRACE	Nelson falls into a deep depression. She goes into a long period of rumination. Her trauma impacts her physical health. Friends and family remind her to keep going and she begins to pick herself up and look forward. Nelson and her husband try to figure out what to do without access to the money the government seized.
Phase 3: EXPLORE	The Nelsons make the heartbreaking decision to move their family thousands of miles away to be near her in-laws. She starts to regain her strength and pushes herself to accomplish small tasks while managing to take care of her children. Despite being in primal survival mode, she remembers that she's a fighter and she's scrappy.
Phase 4: EMERGE	Nelson is still in this phase, but she's had a few wins that make her optimistic for her family's future. She's taken steps toward rebuilding her business. She isn't sure what happens next, but she knows it will involve advocating for civil forfeiture reform.

Erica Taylor Haskins Setback Cycle Snapshot

Phase 1: ESTABLISH	After celebrating ten years in business and defying the odds of being a woman, let alone a Black woman entrepreneur, event planner Erica Taylor Haskins was forced to put her business on pause due to the onset of the Covid-19 pandemic.
Phase 2: EMBRACE	With more free time on her hands, Taylor Haskins remembers staring out her window wondering what was going to happen next. She didn't have the answers, and she wasn't pretending to. She thawed herself out by reflecting on what had happened, what she had learned, and she started to wonder what more she could do. She used her pause to get clear on her values. She helped her peers navigate the PPP loan process so she and other small business owners could try to stay afloat, despite the closures.
Phase 3: EXPLORE	The country's racial reckoning fueled Taylor Haskins' passion even further. She started to explore how to build new experiences centered around activism.
Phase 4: EMERGE	Taylor Haskins found a way to combine her entrepreneurial spirit and event planning industry smarts with her newfound drive for social justice. She started with a new marquee event, "Pizza to the Polls," which encouraged people to vote by creating pop-up pizza parties around polling locations. She sought out other events with a mission-driven tie. If she was going to spend her energy going back to event planning now that the world had reopened, she was going to make a larger societal impact.

Kendall Toole Setback Cycle Snapshot

Phase 1: ESTABLISH	Despite being an overachiever and perfectionist throughout her academic career, Toole struggled with her mental health in private. She tried to "it's fine" her darkness away, using achievement as a cover for her struggles. After a significant mental health episode in college, she sought help from professionals and support from family and friends.
Phase 2: EMBRACE	Toole moved in with her parents and enrolled in intense therapy multiple times a week to process her feelings. Despite taking all the steps to protect herself, she couldn't escape her freeze and fell into rumination. She didn't leave her bed for months.
Phase 3: EXPLORE	She turned to boxing. She found that movement instilled a newfound confidence. Toole used it to work out her anxiety and maintain mental wellness. In fact, her love of boxing prompted her to pursue the sport as a potential career path.
Phase 4: EMERGE	That's what led her to audition at Peloton, where she now leads classes talking openly about her mental health struggles, inspiring and encouraging others to face their demons and work through them.

Robin Arzón Setback Cycle Snapshot

Phase 1: ESTABLISH	Arzón was diagnosed with diabetes just weeks before switching careers from lawyer to fitness instructor. She was also training to run an ultramarathon.
Phase 2: EMBRACE	She faced her situation head on. Yes, she was disappointed, but she acknowledged her disappointment. She didn't ignore it. She embraced movement, as always, to process what she was going through. And she also didn't let it define her identity. Even with her new diagnosis, Arzón was determined to reach that goal of becoming a fitness instructor and ultramarathoner.
Phase 3: EXPLORE	Arzón and other diabetics need to make what she says are "one hundred little decisions every day" to maintain good health. Tapping into her determination and perseverance, she put her insulin patch on while diving into research. She didn't want to simply function; she wanted to thrive. She figured out what she now needed to do every day to live the full life she wanted, even with her condition.
Phase 4: EMERGE	Arzón defied societal expectations of what a fitness instructor or athlete can be. She decided to talk openly during classes about how she worked through her diagnosis in the hopes of inspiring others. She now encourages those in her wellness community to consider how they might be able to apply this to their own lives and "break the boxes they put you in."

Cyrus Veyssi Setback Cycle Snapshot

Phase 1: ESTABLISH	Veyssi began filming funny videos of their sweet, loving, and sometimes awkward interactions with the rest of their family, which, because of their gender nonconformity, led to bullying and online hate. This triggered the memory of being teased as a young child. Veyssi took down some of their posts and hid for a bit.
Phase 2: EMBRACE	Veyssi questioned whether to continue being so public on social media and paused to consider why the often anonymous criticism bothered them so much. During their thaw out, Veyssi's growth mindset enabled them to come to the realization that most people were simply projecting their own insecurities and expectations of what those born as a certain gender should act like, look like, dress like, and more. Veyssi reframed how they thought about the criticisms, and decided to use how they responded as an opportunity to demonstrate compassion and honesty.
Phase 3: EXPLORE	Veyssi stopped taking the insults personally. As they began to share more about their loving family with confidence and grace, the attention and support poured in. They garnered hundreds of thousands of fans on TikTok and Instagram, and the love began to overpower the hate.
Phase 4: EMERGE	They reached new levels of fame, appearing often as the first nonbinary model in makeup and skincare campaigns. They hope to reach kids who, like their childhood self, are still struggling to figure out their identity. They continue to explore more ways to advocate for inclusion, showing what can happen when one chooses to celebrate their identity rather than hide it.

Stacy London Setback Cycle Snapshot

Phase 1: ESTABLISH	After years as a lauded fashion icon and TV star, London faced overwhelming rejection in the same places where she'd always found support. At the same time, she experienced confusing physical symptoms while caring for her sick father.
Phase 2: EMBRACE	As she processed the overwhelming grief and pain over her father's death, she got caught in the rumination trap and experienced a freeze. Doctor after doctor told her nothing was wrong. London's intuition, and her body, told her otherwise. She did some research to arrive at what should have been an obvious diagnosis from a medical professional—she was in perimenopause. Applying a growth mindset, London began to think about how to reframe the difficulties she was experiencing as an opportunity.
Phase 3: EXPLORE	London allowed herself to go deep into her Curiosity as she unlocked conversations across menopause and middle age in a way that began to bring these topics to cultural prominence. No stranger to setbacks, London also started to wonder what she could do next if her TV career was truly on pause. Part of her identity was helping people feel good about themselves. London explored how she might do that now by boosting people's self-esteem through solving the lack of candor and education around menopause.
Phase 4: EMERGE	With clear vision and a consistent mission, London took the reins and is looking to change the narrative and experience of women in midlife. In a glorious full-circle moment, her show about midlife and menopause was picked up by Pinterest TV.

Norma Kamali Setback Cycle Snapshot

Phase 1: ESTABLISH	The ceiling literally fell down over Kamali's workstation after she found out about her husband's infidelity and financial transgressions. She decided to walk away from him and the successful business they'd built.
Phase 2: EMBRACE	With only ninety-eight dollars to her name, she had given up everything she had worked for, had no money to show for it, and was at a loss of how to move forward. She certainly fell into rumination and a freeze before harnessing a growth mindset and letting go of blame and shame so she could move forward.
Phase 3: EXPLORE	With her past behind her, Kamali tapped into her unique trendspotting superpower and slowly started designing clothing again. Eventually, she built up enough of an inventory to launch her own business and open a new store—this time called OMO (on my own).
Phase 4: EMERGE	Kamali remains on the cusp of what's about to trend in culture to this day. She continues to defy fashion industry norms by boasting a fifty plus–year career. As a savvy Setback Cycler and trendsetter, she'll be able to handle whatever comes next.

Blessing Adesiyan Setback Cycle Snapshot

Phase 1: ESTABLISH	Adesiyan showed up to her first day of work as a wide-eyed college graduate with an infant on her hip. With no extended family in the country or resources for childcare, she was unsure if she'd be able to create the career she'd worked so hard to break into after all those years of schooling.
Phase 2: EMBRACE	She tried to balance working motherhood by relying on the kindness of neighbors and her parents, who would meet her at airports around the world to pick up her child as she traveled for work. She knew this wasn't sustainable. Applying a growth mindset, she was ready to take the reins and fix this problem others had so carelessly discarded.
Phase 3: EXPLORE	Adesiyan cultivated her Curiosity to address the concerns of other working moms, who, like her, kept running into impossible circumstances trying to balance childcare with work. She drew on her experiences in various workplaces and used her superpower of systems-thinking as a chemical engineer to connect the dots of what companies were willing to offer and what employees truly needed in terms of all care—not just childcare. She turned to her community and was overwhelmed by a groundswell of support. Would it be possible to fix this issue and find a viable solution that would work for everyone?
Phase 4: EMERGE	Adesiyan left the corporate world and emerged from her setback to create Mother Honestly, now called MH Work-Life. Now, she works with corporate partners to help their employees make better use of available resources, building systems that work for both companies and employers with caregiving responsibilities.

Kaitlyn Soligan Setback Cycle Snapshot (1 of 2)

Phase 1: ESTABLISH	Kaitlyn Soligan left her friends behind and struggled to find community as she built her new life in Louisville.
Phase 2: EMBRACE	Soligan froze and got caught up in rumination, convinced she could never be happy in Louisville. Her best friend, Nicole Stipp, came to visit frequently. Those visits are what thawed Soligan out. They would move around the city, get fresh air, and familiarize themselves with the area. They toured the city's bourbon and whiskey scenes as part of this thaw. And they couldn't help but notice the experience felt like it was missing something.
Phase 3: EXPLORE	These experiences piqued their Curiosity as they started to ask around to see if others felt the way they had on their own whiskey and bourbon tours around Louisville. Soligan and Stipp knew what their superpowers were—building things from scratch, noticing when experiences weren't inclusive or representative of all groups—and cultivating community.
Phase 4: EMERGE	With a nod to their early, idealistic days in D.C., the duo considered how they could create something to benefit the community in Louisville and address these very homogenous travel and tourism experiences. Stipp decided to make her own big move to Louisville, where the two created Matson & Gilman, a whiskey tourism company catered toward marginalized groups, then expanded to create Trouble Bar—a space for connection and comfort that addressed what Soligan was originally seeking—inclusion, belonging, and community.

Nicole Stipp and Kaitlyn Soligan Setback Cycle Snapshot (2 of 2)

Phase 1: ESTABLISH	Trouble Bar was created as a gathering place in the tradition of public houses to form a community and create a safe space for those who felt unwelcome in other whiskey establishments. But when Soligan and Stipp had to close their bar at the beginning of the pandemic, that safe space was threatened. How could they stay afloat while gathering and the sale of liquor were banned in Louisville for the foreseeable future?
Phase 2: EMBRACE	Stipp and Soligan adjusted their expectations of what they needed to keep the bar afloat, and applied a growth mindset to figure out how they could show up for their community without a physical space.
Phase 3: EXPLORE	They tapped into their superpowers of creativity, coming up with the idea to turn lemons into lemonade. Stipp and Soligan turned their recently purchased juices and mixes into a lemonade stand. They showed up for their community by creating a space for them, and when gathering in that space wasn't allowed, it was their community who showed up for them.
Phase 4: EMERGE	When the world opened back up, Trouble Bar remained a safe place to gather once again. Stipp and Soligan emerged from that period with an even more loyal constellation as they had forged new bonds working through that tough period together. They continue to support their community through the inevitable setbacks that arise, knowing they'll get through whatever comes next—together.

Palak Patel Setback Cycle Snapshot

Phase 1: ESTABLISH	After spending a decade building her visibility as a chef, courting investors, and years of careful planning, Patel's restaurant dreams were crushed in an instant. Everything she had been working toward was gone.
Phase 2: EMBRACE	She flew to her parents' house in Atlanta, meditated, reflected, and paused as she mourned the loss of her big dream. She struggled with her new life in Atlanta as she began to shed her identity as a New Yorker. She resisted embracing the new situation until one day, in her childhood bedroom, she finally "woke up."
Phase 3: EXPLORE	Patel began to dream again. She knew what her superpower was—connecting her community over a love of food. As she was trying to figure out how to parlay that into her next move, she remained adaptable even if "what's next" looked completely different from her original plan. She explored her Curiosity all the way to a new food hall, and in it, an empty food stall that beckoned her.
Phase 4: EMERGE	Patel trusted her intuition and decided to take the leap. She began to lay the foundation of her new life, brick by brick. She opened a food stall in her hometown, bought a house, and put down roots in Atlanta once again. The food stall concept was a new take on plant-based Indian-inspired street food, more casual than her original sit-down restaurant, but it felt exactly right for her. She's also about to publish her debut cookbook that celebrates her favorite recipes. She stayed true to her North Star, and through her comeback, Patel was able to find new, creative ways to share her love of food with the world.

Amanda Goetz Setback Cycle Snapshot

Phase 1: ESTABLISH	After getting married and having kids at a young age, Goetz found that her marriage was not lighting her up the way it used to.
Phase 2: EMBRACE	To work through it, she turned to therapy, as well as other coping tactics such as nightly glasses of wine. She wanted to climb out of rumination, exploring stress relief solutions that didn't involve the grogginess of alcohol, which is what led her to the cannabis industry. She harnessed a growth mindset and began learning about a nascent industry that still had a bit of stigma attached to it.
Phase 3: EXPLORE	Goetz continued working at her corporate job and building House of Wise on the side. As she explored her Curiosity, she navigated the obstacles of building a cannabis company early in the industry's nascency. This prompted her to tap into her superpowers of creativity and problem-solving. Entrepreneurship allowed her to pivot more easily, more frequently, and find new ways to approach work and team building.
Phase 4: EMERGE	She brought on investors, hired a team and created a model that helped women explore their stress, sleep and sexuality—destigmatizing the conversations around mothers and sexuality, the cannabis industry as a whole, and creating a successful, scalable business. After exiting House of Wise and selling it to another company, Goetz is now on to Plan C, which she is certain will involve helping women find new ways to prioritize themselves.

THE SETBACK CYCLE

Cate Luzio Setback Cycle Snapshot

Phase 1: ESTABLISH	After creating Luminary, a space for women at all stages of their career, and seeing a successful first year, Luzio's space was forced to close due to the onset of the pandemic and the stay-at-home orders. People began canceling memberships, unsure about what the future might hold.
Phase 2: EMBRACE	Luzio didn't have time to "it's fine" everything away or deny that she was in a setback. She has always been a realist and a woman of action. She sat in her setback as she worked to address the logistics of her situation. As she battled an early and severe case of Covid, she kept going, even when she perhaps should have rested.
Phase 3: EXPLORE	Drawing on her superpower of confident humility and tapping into her constellation, she enlisted her team to make collective decisions, even when those decisions were extremely tough. As she slowly steered her business forward, she recognized the enormous impact she would still be able to have on women at all stages of their careers all over the world.
Phase 4: EMERGE	Her corporate partners grew concerned about retaining women as they fled the workforce. Luminary was perfectly situated to help. It was time to run through the small-step framework again, going through the same process that led her to create Luminary after leaving her banking career. She did the same to help her partners navigate the next few workplace movements, from the Great Resignation to the recession to the return to office debates. Luzio Emerged from her setback by expanding her reach, and her impact. Two years later, Luminary had expanded to twelve corporate partners and over ten thousand members worldwide.

Endnotes

Introduction

1 datascience@berkeley, "Changing the Curve: Women in Computing," July 14, 2021, https://ischoolonline.berkeley.edu/blog/women-computing-computer-science/#:~:text=The%20proportion%20of%20women%20receiving,bachelor's%20degree%20recipients%20were%20women.

2 "Basal Ganglia," Cleveland Clinic, August 5, 2022, https://my.clevelandclinic.org/health/body/23962-basal-ganglia.

3 Reshma Saujani, "Biden's Childcare Plan Will Work—If Companies Do Their Fair Share," MSNBC, April 20, 2023, https://www.msnbc.com/know-your-value/out-of-office/biden-s-childcare-plan-will-work-if-companies-do-their-n1304503.

Chapter 1

1 Susan David, *Emotional Agility: Get Unstuck, Embrace Change, and Thrive in Work and Life* (New York: Avery/Penguin Random House, 2016).

2 Adam Grant, "Feeling Blah During the Pandemic? It's Called Languishing," *New York Times*, December 3, 2021, https://www.nytimes.com/2021/04/19/well/mind/covid-mental-health-languishing.html

3 Jena McGregor, "The Leadership Lessons in Sheryl Sandberg's and Adam Grant's New Book About Resilience and Grief," *Washington Post*, April 25, 2017, https://www.washingtonpost.com/news/on-leadership/wp/2017/04/25/the-leadership-lessons-in-sheryl-sandbergs-and-adam-grants-new-book-about-resiliency-and-grief/.

4 Paul Carrol and Chunka Mui, "Seven Ways to Fail Big," *Harvard Business Review* (September 2008), https://hbr.org/2008/09/seven-ways-to-fail-big.

5 Adam Grant (@AdamMGrant), "We don't need to celebrate failure. We do need to make it safe to admit failure—that's how we learn from mistakes," Tweet, April 27, 2017, 7:46 a.m., https://twitter.com/adammgrant/status/857576733737922561.

6 Grant, "Bouncing Back from Rejection," LinkedIn article, April 22, 2019, https://www.linkedin.com/pulse/bouncing-back-from-rejection-adam-grant/.

7 Grant, *Think Again: The Power of Knowing What You Don't Know* (Viking: New York, 2021).

8 Guy Raz, James Delahoussaye, and Jeff Rogers, "Live from the HIBT Summit: Adam Grant," August 19, 2021, in *How I Built This*, produced by James Delahoussaye, podcast, 51:00, https://www.npr.org/2021/08/18/1028826501/live-from-the-hibt-summit-adam-grant.

9 David, 70.

10 David, 66.

11 Grant, *Think Again.*

12 Claire Cain Miller, "The Motherhood Penalty vs. the Fatherhood Bonus," *The New York Times*, September 6, 2014, https://www.nytimes.com/2014/09/07/upshot/a-child-helps-your-career-if-youre-a-man.html.

13 Claudia Goldin, Sari Pekkala Kerr, and Claudia Olivetti, "When the Kids Grow Up: Women's Employment and Earnings across the Family Cycle," National Bureau of Economic Research working paper, August 2022, https://www.nber.org/papers/w30323.

14 Sandra Florian, "Becoming a Mother Reduces a Woman's Earning Potential by up to 10 Percent per Child," PennToday, November 20, 2018, https://penntoday.upenn.edu/news/becoming-mother-reduces-womans-earning-potential-10-per-cent-child.

15 Kathy Gurchiek, "The Wage Gap Is Wider for Working Mothers," SHRM, October 21, 2019, https://www.shrm.org/resourcesandtools/hr-topics/compensation/pages/wage-gap-is-wider-for-working-mothers.aspx.

16 Erin Eatough, "Suffering in Silence: Why Working Parents Hide Child Care Woes from Their Employers," BetterUp, March 10, 2022, https://www.betterup.com/blog/suffering-in-silence-why-working-parents-hide-child-care-woes-from-their-employers?utm_source=substack&utm_medium=email.

17 Allyson Felix, "Allyson Felix: My Own Nike Pregnancy Story," *New York Times*, May 22, 2019, https://www.nytimes.com/2019/05/22/opinion/allyson-felix-pregnancy-nike.html.

18 Cathy Cassata, "All About Disenfranchised Grief," PsychCentral, July 28, 2021, https://psychcentral.com/health/disenfranchised-grief#what-it-is.

19 Audrey Goodson Kingo, "Companies Need More Than Good Benefits to Support Parents Returning from Leave," *Mother Honestly*, March 30, 2023, https://www.newsletter.mhworklife.com/p/companies-need-more-than-good-benefits.

20 Amy Shoenthal, "Will the Future of Co-Working Spaces Rely on the Hospitality Industry? The Women Rebuilding The Riveter Think So," *Forbes*, March 29, 2022, https://www.forbes.com/sites/amyshoenthal/2022/03/29/will-the-future-of-co-working-spaces-rely-on-the-hospitality-industry-the-women-rebuilding-the-riveter-think-so/?sh=212196ae19a0.

Endnotes

21 Domeneco Montanaro, "Poll: Americans Want Abortion Restrictions, but Not as Far as Red States Are Going," NPR, April 26, 2023, https://www.npr.org/2023/04/26/1171863775/poll-americans-want-abortion-restrictions-but-not-as-far-as-red-states-are-going#:~:text=Support%20for%20abortion%20rights%20at,last%2020%20years%20or%20so.

Chapter 2

1 Courtney E. Ackerman, "What Is Positive Psychology and Why Is It Important?" *Positive Psychology*, April 20, 2018, https://positivepsychology.com/what-is-positive-psychology-definition/.

2 David, 2.

3 Richard Sima, "Why Do We Get Our Best Ideas in the Shower?" *Washington Post*, January 12, 2023, https://www.washingtonpost.com/wellness/2023/01/12/shower-thoughts-creativity-brain/.

4 Zachary C. Irving, Catherine McGrath, Lauren Flynn, Aaron Glasser, and Caitlin Mills, "The Shower Effect: Mand Wandering Facilitates Creative Incubation During Moderately Engaging Activities," *Psychology of Aesthetics, Creativity, and the Arts* (September 2022), https://psycnet.apa.org/doiLanding?doi=10.1037%2Faca0000516.

5 "Intrepid (CV-11)," Naval History and Heritage Command, https://www.history.navy.mil/browse-by-topic/ships/aircraft-carriers/uss-intrepid.html#:~:text=A%20few%20days%20later%2C%20aircraft,as%20a%20museum%20was%20successful.

6 Loren Schweniger, "The Roots of Enterprise: Black-Owned Businesses in Virginia, 1830-1880," *The Virginia Magazine of History and Biography* 100, no. 4 (October 1992): 515–542, https://www.jstor.org/stable/4249312.

7 Barbara Orbach Natanson, "Exploring Black-Owned Businesses from the Turn of the 20th Century," Library of Congress, August 11, 2021, https://blogs.loc.gov/picturethis/2021/08/exploring-black-owned-businesses-from-the-turn-of-the-20th-century/.

8 Donna Kelley, Mahdi Majbouri, and Angela Randolph, "Black Women Are More Likely to Start a Business than White Men," *Harvard Business Review*, May 11, 2021, https://hbr.org/2021/05/black-women-are-more-likely-to-start-a-business-than-white-men.

9 Rachel Sheppard, "Only 3% of Business Investment Goes to Women, and That's a Problem for Everyone," crunchbase, April 8, 2020, https://about.crunchbase.com/blog/business-investment-to-women/.

10 Ashley Bittner and Brigette Lau, "Women-Led Startups Received Just 2.3% of VC Funding in 2020," *Harvard Business Review*, February 25, 2021, https://hbr.org/2021/02/women-led-startups-received-just-2-3-of-vc-funding-in-2020#:~:text=In%202019%2C%202.8%25%20of%20funding,this%20precipitous%20drop%20are%20clear.

11 Timothy Carter, "The True Failure Rate of Small Businesses," *Entrepreneur*, January 3, 2021, https://www.entrepreneur.com/starting-a-business/the-true-failure-rate-of-small-businesses/361350#:~:text=According%20to%20data%20from%20the,about%20half%20will%20have%20failed.

12 Emily Nagoski and Amelia Nagoski, *Burnout* (Ballantine Books: New York, 2019).

13 Nagoski and Nagoski.

14 Susan Cain, *Bittersweet: How Sorrow and Longing Make Us Whole* (Crown: New York, 2022), 53.

15 Cain.

Chapter 3

1 988 Suicide & Crisis Lifeline, https://988lifeline.org/.

2 "Understanding the Stress Response," *Harvard Health Publishing*, July 6, 2020, https://www.health.harvard.edu/staying-healthy/understanding-the-stress-response.

3 "Understanding the Stress Response."

4 Shoenthal, "Robin Arzón on Coming Back from Maternity Leave: The Myth of Balance and the Power of No," *Forbes*, August 17, 2021, https://www.forbes.com/sites/amyschoenberger/2021/08/17/robin-arzn-on-coming-back-from-maternity-leave-the-myth-of-balance-and-the-power-of-no/?sh=66e6cd926a69.

5 Morra Aarons-Mele, "What Drives You to Achieve? Linkedin, September 21, 2022, https://www.linkedin.com/pulse/what-drives-you-achieve-morra-aarons-mele/.

6 Aarons-Mele.

7 Aarons-Mele.

8 David, 74.

9 Aarons-Mele.

Chapter 4

1 Carol S. Dweck, *Mindset: The New Psychology of Success* (Ballantine: New York, 2006).

2 DGAF = don't give a fuck

3 Dweck.

4 Chantel Prat, *The Neuroscience of You: How Every Brain Is Different and How to Understand Yours* (Dutton: New York, 2022), 35.

5 Dweck.

6 Dweck.

7 "Fact Sheet: Biden-Harris Administration Advances Equality and Visibility for Transgender Americans," White House, March 31, 2022, https://www.whitehouse.gov/briefing-room/statements-releases/2022/03/31/fact-sheet-biden-harris-administration-advances-equality-and-visibility-for-transgender-americans/.

Endnotes

8 Alex Nguyen and William Melhado, "Gov. Gregg Abbott Signs Legislation Barring Trans Youth from Accessing Transition-Related Care," *Texas Tribune*, June 2, 2023, https://www.texastribune.org/2023/06/02/texas-gender-affirming-care-ban/#:~:text=Gov.,new%20law%20from%20taking%20effect.

9 Grant, "Bouncing Back from Rejection," April 2019, in Worklife, podcast, 44:52, https://open.spotify.com/episode/3kPX80bSXoq8q6enuhfx0p?si=jwER-jo-0Qla1zoTZ3GnjbA&dl_branch=1&nd=1.

10 Grant (/in/adammgrant), "If you punish people for being wrong, they cover up their mistakes. They make excuses and throw blame to justify the past. If you treat being wrong as a learning opportunity, people admit their errors. They take responsibility for correcting and preventing them in the future." LinkedIn post/infographic, 2021, https://www.linkedin.com/posts/adammgrant_if-you-punish-people-for-being-wrong-they-activity-6776542703112003584-2mvf/.

11 Prat, 186.

12 Prat, 193.

Chapter 5

1 Leon F. Seltzer, "Curiosity Is Invaluable: Can We Lose It as We Age?" *Psychology Today*, July 5, 2023, https://www.psychologytoday.com/au/blog/evolution-of-the-self/202306/curiosity-is-invaluable-can-we-lose-it-as-we-age.

2 Francesca Gino, "The Business Case for Curiosity," *Harvard Business Review* (September–October 2018), https://hbr.org/2018/09/the-business-case-for-curiosity.

3 Darcy Banco et al., "Sex and Race Differences in the Evaluation and Treatment of Young Adults Presenting to the Emergency Department with Chest Pain," *Journal of the American Heart Association* 11, no. 10 (May 4, 2022), https://www.ahajournals.org/doi/10.1161/JAHA.121.024199?itid=lk_inline_enhanced-template.

4 Nancy N. Maserejian, Carol L. Link, Karen L. Lutfey, Lisa D. Marceau, and John B. McKinlay, "Disparities in Physicians' Interpretations of Heart Disease Symptoms by Patient Gender: Results of a Video Vignette Factorial Experiment," *Journal of Women's Health* 18, no. 10 (2009), https://www.ncbi.nlm.nih.gov/pmc/articles/PMC2825679/pdf/jwh.2008.1007.pdf.

5 Stacy London, "Stacy London's Post-Pandemic Pivot Was Inspired by a Mistake She Made Earlier in Her Career," *Fast Company*, January 5, 2023, https://www.fastcompany.com/90829965/stacy-london-career-advice.

6 Grant, "Bouncing Back from Rejection."

7 Grant, "Bouncing Back from Rejection."

8 Susan Dominus, "Women Have Been Misled About Menopause," *New York Times*, June 15, 2023, https://www.nytimes.com/2023/02/01/magazine/menopause-hot-flashes-hormone-therapy.html.

9 Lisa Selin Davis, "Why Modern Medicine Keeps Overlooking Menopause," *New York Times*, April 6, 2021, https://www.nytimes.com/2021/04/06/us/menopause-perimenopause-symptoms.html.

10 Reenita Das, "Menopause Unveils Itself as the Next Big Opportunity in Femtech," *Forbes*, July 24, 2019, https://www.forbes.com/sites/reenitadas/2019/07/24/menopause-unveils-itself-as-the-next-big-opportunity-in-femtech/?sh=5862cc9a6535.

11 Amy Larocca, "Welcome to the Menopause Gold Rush," *New York Times*, December 20, 2022, https://www.nytimes.com/2022/12/20/style/menopause-womens-health-goop.html.

Chapter 6

1 Raz, "Norma Kamali: Norma Kamali," February 2021, on How I Built This, produced by Guy Raz, podcast, 88:08, https://podcasts.apple.com/us/podcast/norma-kamali-norma-kamali/id1150510297?i=1000507255597.

2 Raz.

3 Raz.

4 Gwen Moran, "How to Find Your Superpower," *Fast Company*, https://www.fastcompany.com/40578240/how-to-find-your-superpower.

5 Care.com Editorial Staff, "This Is How Much Childcare Costs in 2023," Care, June 13, 2023, https://www.care.com/c/how-much-does-child-care-cost/.

6 Lucy Danley, "Over Half of Families are Spending More Than 20% of Income on Child Care," First Five Years Fund, June 29, 2022, https://www.ffyf.org/over-half-of-families-are-spending-more-than-20-on-child-care/.

7 Olivia Konotey-Ahulu, "UK Mothers Say It No Longer Makes Financial Sense to Work," Bloomberg, March 1, 2023, https://www.bloomberg.com/news/articles/2023-03-02/uk-mothers-say-it-no-longer-makes-financial-sense-to-work?srnd=premium&sref=AGYpi2Ba&tpcc=nlbroadsheet#xj4y7vzkg.

8 Shoenthal, "A Future of Work that Includes Care Starts with a 'Work-Life Wallet' to Support Individual Employee Needs," *Forbes*, November 16, 2022, https://www.forbes.com/sites/amyshoenthal/2022/11/16/a-future-of-work-that-includes-care-starts-with-a-work-life-wallet-to-support-individual-employee-needs/?sh=1372ca157cb8.

9 Shoenthal, "A Future of Work."

10 Shoenthal, "A Future of Work."

11 Shoenthal, "A Future of Work."

12 Shoenthal, "A Future of Work."

13 Shoenthal, "A Future of Work."

Endnotes

14 Anne Trafton, "How the Brain Controls Our Habits," MIT News, October 29, 2012, https://news.mit.edu/2012/understanding-how-brains-control-our-habits-1029.

Chapter 7

1 Nagoski and Nagoski, 133.

2 John Leland, "How Loneliness Is Damaging Our Health," *New York Times*, April 20, 2022, https://www.nytimes.com/2022/04/20/nyregion/loneliness-epidemic.html.

3 Susan McPherson with Jackie Ashton, *The Lost Art of Connecting: The Gather, Ask, Do Method for Building Meaningful Business Relationships* (New York: McGraw-Hill, 2021), xiii.

4 Fred Minnick, "Women's History Month Spotlight: Women Bootleggers," *HuffPost*, March 10, 2014, https://www.huffpost.com/entry/womens-history-month-spot_b_4927284.

5 "Montana's Whiskey Women: Female Bootleggers During Prohibition," *Montana Women's History*, January 16, 2014, http://montanawomenshistory.org/montanas-whiskey-women-female-bootleggers-during-prohibition/.

6 Daniel Pink, "The Science of Regret," October 5, 2022, on A Slight Change of Plans, October 5, 2022, podcast, 42:25, https://www.youtube.com/watch?v=AWRYIJn2Sss.

7 "Understanding the Stress Response."

8 Tara John, "How the World's First Loneliness Minister Will Tackle 'the Sad Reality of Modern Life,'" *Time*, April 25, 2018, https://time.com/5248016/tracey-crouch-uk-loneliness-minister/.

9 Matt Lloyd, "'Happy to Chat' Benches: The Woman Getting Strangers to Talk," BBC, October 19, 2019, https://www.bbc.com/news/uk-wales-50000204.

10 Erik Brynjolfsson et al., "The Real Strength of Weak Ties," *Stanford News*, September 15, 2022, https://news.stanford.edu/2022/09/15/real-strength-weak-ties/.

11 Aprile Rickert, "Kentucky Voters Reject Amendment that Would Have Affirmed No Right to Abortion," NPR, November 9, 2022, https://www.npr.org/2022/11/09/1134835022/kentucky-abortion-amendment-midterms-results.

Chapter 8

1 Nagoski and Nagoski.

2 Nagoski and Nagoski, 35.

Chapter 9

1 "Booming Cannabis Market to Hit USD 197.74 Billion by 2028," GlobeNews-wire, May 12, 2023, https://www.globenewswire.com/en/news-release/2023/05/12/2667625/0/en/Booming-Cannabis-Market-to-Hit-USD-197-74-Billion-by-2028-An-Overview-of-the-Fastest-Growing-Marijuana-Industry.html.

Chapter 10

1 Angela Duckworth, *Grit: The Power of Passion and Perseverance* (New York: Scribner, 2016).

2 Matthew J. Bundick, "The Benefits of Reflecting on and Discussing Purpose in Life in Emerging Adulthood," New Dir Youth Dev, no. 132 (Winter 2011): 89–103, https://pubmed.ncbi.nlm.nih.gov/22275281/.

3 Patrick Van Kessel and Adam Hughes, "Americans Who Find Meaning in These Four Areas Have Higher Life Satisfaction," Pew Research Center, November 20, 2018, https://www.pewresearch.org/fact-tank/2018/11/20/americans-who-find-meaning-in-these-four-areas-have-higher-life-satisfaction/.

4 Aliza Licht, "How 'Whisper Networks' Can Help You Leverage Negotiating and Your Career," *New York Post*, February 23, 2020, https://nypost.com/2020/02/23/how-whisper-networks-can-help-you-leverage-negotiating-and-your-career/.

5 Melissa Wiley, "An Executive Who Worked in Banking for 20 Years Quit Her Job to Found a Female-Focused Members Space in New York City. I Spent a Day There to See if I Would Pay $150 a Month for It — Here's What It's Like," *Business Insider*, January 15, 2020, https://www.businessinsider.com/luminary-nyc-women-collaboration-hub-membership-coworking-networking-social-space-2020-1#one-of-my-favorite-details-was-this-pair-of-books-sandwiched-between-pineapple-bookends-in-the-largest-conference-room-16.

6 Leslie Feinzaig, "All I Want for International Women's Day: No More Female Founder Takedowns," *Fast Company*, March 8, 2023, https://www.fastcompany.com/90861837/international-womens-day-no-more-female-founder-takedowns?utm_source=substack&utm_medium=email&fbclid=PAAabyUWWAMMkzdwPEFgeVyhIPGikbPAXU_YdNogn0-_v8FTRl-LAkUggsj1_g.

7 Grant, Think Again.

8 Taylor Francis Online, The Great Resignation in the United States: A Study of Labor Market Segmentation, https://www.tandfonline.com/doi/abs/10.1080/07360932.2022.2164599.

9 Cate Luzio (/in/cluzio), "The key to physical health, mental health, and longevity..." LinkedIn post, February 2023, https://www.linkedin.com/posts/cluzio_essay-the-lifelong-power-of-close-relationships-activity-7024381749086314496-yfnX/?originalSubdomain=et.

Endnotes

Conclusion

1 Grant (adamgrant), "Not every difficult experience is trauma ..." Instagram photo, February 13, 2023, https://www.instagram.com/p/ConHSLYphGT/.

2 "National Business Coalition for Childcare," Moms First, https://momsfirst.us/childcare-coalition/.

3 Aarons-Mele.

Acknowledgments

On March 25, 2021, I called my friend Ruthie Ackerman and shared the seeds of an idea I had been thinking about for years. I will never forget her response. Thank you, Ruthie, for helping so many authors bring their visions to life, and thank you for being the first person to say, "Yes, this should absolutely be a book."

Courtney Paganelli, you are a goddamn force within the publishing industry and I still can't believe I am lucky enough to call you my agent. You constantly go above and beyond what's expected of your role, acting as my advocate, therapist, editor, and hypewoman. (And therapist again.) I could not be more grateful for you.

Adriana Senior, I can't thank you enough for bringing me into the Regalo Press family, for seeing the potential of this book before most of it was written, and for working with me to bring *The Setback Cycle* into the world.

Gretchen Young, thank you so much for creating Regalo Press. You are a true gift to the entire publishing world and it has been an honor to work with you.

Courtney Allison, thank you for tiptoeing back into the world of book publishing to give this manuscript, and the proposal that came before it, a fresh perspective. And thank you to Taylor Swift for performing at Courtney's birthday party, for her and 20,000 other fans.

Shoshanna Hecht, Chantel Prat, Susan McPherson, Adam Grant, Roshan Shah, Morra Aarons-Mele, Michelle Casarella—thank you

Acknowledgments

for lending your expertise so that I, and readers, could gain a deeper understanding of how setbacks work. Thank you for agreeing to let me interview you, often several times, despite your busy schedules, despite being pulled in a million directions. I will never be able to express my full gratitude.

To those who generously let me share so many details about their stories, I hope I did you justice on these pages. Reshma Saujani, Stacy London, Erica Taylor, Robin Arzón, Kendall Toole, Norma Kamali, Blessing Adesiyan, Amy Nelson, Amanda Goetz, Cyrus Veyssi, Palak Patel, Nicole Stipp, Kaitlyn Soligan and Cate Luzio, I continue to be amazed by all of you, and you all are the reason I wrote this book. I hope your stories inspire and motivate others in the same way you inspired and motivated me throughout this entire journey. Thank you, thank you, thank you.

Courtney, Drew, and Penni were among this book's earliest supporters, from reading chapters after Barry White yoga to helping each other through some of our darker periods. Everyone should be so lucky to discover lifelong friendship while shooting carrots from a bra slingshot through a sunroof.

Thank you Aylin for always finding new ways to celebrate every small milestone in your friends' lives. Every time I made the slightest small accomplishment on the journey of writing this book, from finishing some version of a proposal to meeting a word count goal, some sort of gift or plant arrived at my door.

Vanessa, you are an inspiration for gift giving and hosting. Thank you for being so thoughtful and for always going out of your way to celebrate the milestones in women's lives that don't include weddings or child rearing.

I am so grateful for the professional women's organizations I've been lucky to be a part of, from Luminary to The Li.st, the Entreprenista League, the Riveter and more. Being around the inspirational women in these communities gave me the courage, motivation, and support I needed to embark on this writing journey.

Jessica Abo, you are the best hype person anyone could ask for. You are also incredibly thoughtful, brilliant, and compassionate, and I am so lucky our paths crossed.

I'm lucky enough to have an incredible constellation of supportive friends, from the Joy Squad to the Hustlers, the Tangerines, the Park Moms, the Beach Besties, the Ryan Phillipe slash Penn Badgely fan club and the Sunnyside moms. Our groups have weird names but they are my absolute lifeline for advice, rants, silliness, and security.

To all the bosses, managers, and mentors who I've worked with over the years, especially Adrianna Bevilaqua and Alex Nicholson, thank you for helping me work through some of my most difficult yet transformational career setbacks—and triumphs.

One of the biggest luxuries I had while writing this book was access to reliable childcare. Nanny Beth, you are the best third parent, Matt, Cory, and I could ever have asked for. I am deeply grateful to you, and to Alex, who took care of Cory when she was a baby. The work you did so that I could do this work is beyond appreciated. Thank you both for everything.

Family is the most important thing in the world, and I won the lottery with mine.

I was raised by two of the most creative people I know—an artist and a musician who made sure their children grew into adulthood with confidence, security, and incredibly strong work ethics. Mom and Dad, thank you for raising us to be independent, for encouraging us to use our voices, for inspiring both of us to pursue our big dreams, but also for keeping us grounded. Every day I aspire to your level of parenting, and to raise your granddaughter as you raised me.

And mom, thank you for reading this book 100 times. You truly demonstrate love and support through candor and honesty, which is not always easy to do. It's one of the many things I admire about you.

Lisa, I'm so lucky to share the bond of sisterhood with you, especially as we grow into our more "seasoned" years. Thank you for continuing that sisterhood into the next generation with the best little cousin trio.

When people decide to get married, they can never predict what lies ahead, but Matt, I continue to be amazed by our incredible partnership in ways I never could have imagined. Thank you for motivating me to aim higher in every way, and for pushing me to do all the big, scary, exciting things, even when that meant you had to take on a larger share of the work at home. Thank you for being so patient with me during my many moments of indecisiveness, both about this book and in life. I keep finding new levels of admiration for you every single day. I love you so much.

Cory, you are the reason for everything I do. I'm certain that this world has the potential to be so much better and I am determined to do everything in my power to make that happen. I want you to live a beautiful life of your own design, on your own terms, without limit. You know exactly who you are and I hope you never lose sight of that as you cycle through whatever setbacks life throws at you. You are the best kid on the planet and I love the person you're becoming. I am so proud of you.

About the Author

Amy Shoenthal is a renowned journalist, author, and marketing consultant. As a contributor to *ForbesWomen* and *Harvard Business Review*, she shines the spotlight on those who have been historically underestimated yet are doing the work to solve society's biggest problems. Her work has included interviews with a wide range of leaders such as Senator Mazie Hirono, Tracee Ellis Ross, Tory Burch, and more.

Amy also boasts a two-decade marketing career, working with some of the world's largest brands, from Procter & Gamble to Google. She now works with founders, corporations, nonprofits and small businesses to shape their brand narratives and captivate audiences through strategic storytelling. After completing *The Setback Cycle*, she began working with organizations to help their employees and managers confidently lead through tumultuous times, offering the tools to help their teams navigate their own inevitable setbacks together.

Amy graduated from The University of Maryland's journalism school. Her children's book, *A Magical Day in Sunnyside*, is a tribute to the independent-owned businesses in her own beloved neighborhood of Sunnyside, Queens, where she lives with her husband and daughter.